# TIM SCHMOYER

## life in student ministry
### Practical Conversations on Thriving in Youth Ministry

Good, proven, practical ideas for youth ministry can be hard to come by. This book is loaded! I couldn't put it down! Whether you are brand-new, just-out-of-the-box to youth ministry or a well-weathered veteran, there is something here for you. I especially loved the blog style multiple perspectives from experienced youth workers on every topic.

**—Matt McAlack, Director of Youth Ministry Program, Philadelphia Biblical University**

If you're thinking about going into youth ministry, just starting, or in your first few years as a youth pastor, this book is a must-read for you. In a collaborative format Tim not only speaks from his personal experiences but draws on the collective wisdom of many other seasoned youth ministry veterans who add perspective, advice, and ideas in each chapter.

**—Tic Long, Executive Director, Youth Specialties**

Real, reliable, and relevant is the best way to describe this must-read book for anyone involved in youth ministry! Tim's book shares heartfelt and life-changing conversations that will challenge and refresh you! This book is in my top three of hundreds of ministry books in my office!

**—E. J. Swanson, nationally recognized Christian youth speaker**

In the past twenty years much has been written about youth ministry: resource books about *how* to do it, theological books about *why* to do it, sociological books about the *need* for it, even books about what it will look like in another twenty years. Tim's book isn't any of those and yet is all of them. In real life you can't choose to separate the different parts of youth ministry. You have to be at the same time a theologian, sociologist, game leader, bus driver, counselor, pastor, and friend. Tim navigates all these worlds—and does a great job of getting others to join him—in putting together a book that is practical, theological, missiological, whimsical, contemporary, and future focused.

**—Lars Rood, author, *Youth Ministry on a Shoestring***

In this digital age with all of its influences and distractions, impacting teenagers for Christ is harder than ever. Springboarding off of his blog, his own personal growth as a youth minister, and the voices of other youth workers, Tim has produced a very practical handbook for anyone working with students. As a parent of a teenager myself, I am so glad for leaders like Tim reaching out to this generation.

**—George Hillman, Associate Professor of Spiritual Formation and Leadership, Dallas Theological Seminary**

Tim brings an entourage of wisdom to the table with this unique book, sharing not only his own youth ministry insight but also a swarm of experienced veterans offering a pleasant whipped topping to his tasty caramel macchiato.

**—Jonathan McKee, President, The Source for Youth Ministry**

Most books (about youth ministry or any subject) are one-way communication from the author to the reader. Tim's practical book on youth ministry adds a couple dimensions to that approach, by bringing in dozens of other voices in response to Tim's thoughts and suggestions. A youth ministry book as dialogue—what a great idea!

**—Mark Oestreicher, speaker, author, consultant**

*Life in Student Ministry* relays practical conversations designed to help you build a solid youth ministry vision and gives you tactical insights for getting it done. Tim Schmoyer hits the bull's eye as he challenges youth leaders to prayerfully minister out of a love for God that is so deep it becomes contagious to teenagers. Tim's candid observations will help you cultivate a ministry where students are growing deeper in their walk with God while going wider into their world with the message of the gospel.

**—Greg Stier, Founder and President, Dare 2 Share Ministries**

Here's a great resource for youth leaders who are seeking to enhance their ministry. What I love about Tim is that he is bubbling with practical ideas. He is a practitioner who has made his share of mistakes and learned from experience. Reading this book gives you the opportunity to glean the best thoughts from a group of seasoned ministers.

**—Seth Barnes, President, Adventures In Missions**

Tim's book ought to be on the shelf of every youth leader! He takes us beyond the textbook theories of the classroom and gives us practical examples he's learned by personal experience as a youth pastor. This is not a bird's eye view of youth ministry; Tim writes from the trenches, with a heart focused on God and hands reaching out to a generation of students. Put this one on your must-read list.

**—Dave Huizing, local church missionary, Word of Life**

As a mentor on the LISM Mentor Team, I intend to recommend, no, gently push, every mentee to read this valuable resource. This book is a must-read for any youth worker, whether they are just getting started or have been in ministry for years. It's like having a LISM Mentor right by your side and at your fingertips.

**—Brian Ford, veteran youth pastor, LISM Mentor**

I have watched Tim over the years become one of the top leaders in youth ministry. Whether you are in youth ministry full time, part time, or as a volunteer, this book is a must-read. Tim knows where youth ministry has been, where it is now, and what the future looks like. Technology is reaching this generation like never before and is changing these teenagers every year. Thank God for a leader like Tim who is leading the charge in reaching this generation and training youth leaders.

**—Bill Scott, President, Free Our Family**

This book provides practical insight into the world of student ministry for any student pastor or youth worker. I love the dialogue Tim has created from using multiple voices.

**—Brad Cooper, youth pastor, NewSpring Community Church**

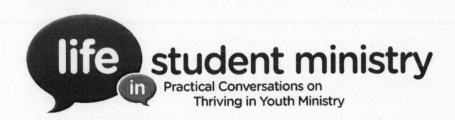

**life** **in** **student ministry**
Practical Conversations on
Thriving in Youth Ministry

TIM SCHMOYER

# life in student ministry

Practical Conversations on
Thriving in Youth Ministry

youth
specialties

ZONDERVAN.com/
AUTHORTRACKER
*follow your favorite authors*

ZONDERVAN

*Life in Student Ministry*
Copyright © 2011 by Tim Schmoyer

YS Youth Specialties is a trademark of YOUTHWORKS!, INCORPORATED and is registered with the United States Patent and Trademark Office.

This title is also available as a Zondervan ebook. Visit www.zondervan.com/ebooks.

Requests for information should be addressed to:

Zondervan, *Grand Rapids, Michigan 49530*

Library of Congress Cataloging-in-Publication Data

Schmoyer, Tim.
    Life in student ministry : practical conversations on thriving in youth ministry /
Tim Schmoyer.
        p.   cm.
    ISBN  978-0-310-32909-1 (softcover)
    1. Church work with youth.  I. Title.
BV4447.S2855 2010
259'.23—dc22                                                                2010044316

*Cover design: Toolbox Studios*
*Interior design: David Conn*

*Printed in the United States of America*

11  12  13  14  15  16  /DCI/  20  19  18  17  16  15  14  13  12  11  10  9  8  7  6  5  4  3  2  1

# Contents

## chapter 4: Sharing God's Word with Teens

## chapter 5: When Teens and Parents Won't Commit to the Youth Ministry

## chapter 6: Communication

## chapter 7: Managing Money

## chapter 8: Finding Adult Volunteers

# chapter 9: Once Your Volunteers Are in Place

# chapter 10: Challenges You May Face in Youth Ministry

## chapter 11: Ways to Make Youth Ministry Easier

## chapter 12: Serving in Youth Ministry for the Long Haul

## Conclusion

## Acknowledgments

# Introduction

In the summer of 2005, I found myself sitting alone in my small apartment, bored and not sure how to use my time. I had just graduated from seminary, and the homework load that had consumed my time was gone. I was serving in a youth ministry position at a local church, but it was only part time and left me with a chunk of available space in my schedule. I wasn't sure what to do with this time—the video games that had once attracted me had strangely lost their appeal.

As I was mindlessly surfing the Web one evening, I discovered that my name was available as a .com domain. I decided to register it and start a little blog. I had no vision for the website, I just thought it would be fun to see what happened.

The first several weeks I wrote about things only my mom would care about, such as the pizza I had reheated three times and my subsequent stomachaches. But as I continued to blog, I couldn't help but write about my passion: youth ministry. I started reading other youth workers' blogs as well, and I discovered that we were all sharing about our struggles, joys, successes, and failures in youth ministry. We would think out loud with one another by commenting on blog posts—this allowed us to respond to each other's thoughts and give feedback. I quickly learned that the online community of youth ministry bloggers would be a very key tool in continuing my education and sharpening my youth ministry skills.

The title of my blog became Life In Student Ministry, and now the site contains several years of content for youth ministry leaders. While it tends to fluctuate between the practical and philosophical aspects of youth ministry, this book is an attempt to bring together a collection of useful how-to posts from a wide range of youth ministry topics.

What I'm most excited about in this book are the snippets of conversations and comments that surround my content. As I've discovered through blogging, I have a lot to learn from the people who surround me. The other voices in this book are intended to keep some of the conversational tone of blogging intact and to give you some different perspectives on what I communicate here. I've learned a great deal from many of these youth workers and I hope you do, too!

Although much of the material in this book is applicable to many ministry contexts, please don't take any of this content as a prescription for your ministry. There is no one-size-fits-all youth ministry program box that can be shipped to any ministry.

This book contains many ideas and a lot of advice, but it does not comprehensively address these how-to issues. Think of this as a starting point and a look into some of my online conversations concerning these youth ministry topics rather than a complete approach to youth ministry.

When in doubt about how to proceed with a struggle or issue in your youth ministry, I've learned that it's best to surround yourself with a host of godly influences (both online and in real life) who can talk with you and will help you process through some of the challenges in your ministry.

If you like this book, you'll probably enjoy reading my blog at www.studentministry.org since most of this content was originally published there over the past couple years. Visit www.studentministry.org for information on how you can subscribe to the Life In Student Ministry blog to get more articles like these delivered to you electronically.

I pray the information in this book will encourage you, equip you, support you, and enable you to serve the Lord more effectively as you serve the wonderful teenagers he's entrusted to you. God bless!

Tim Schmoyer
www.studentministry.org

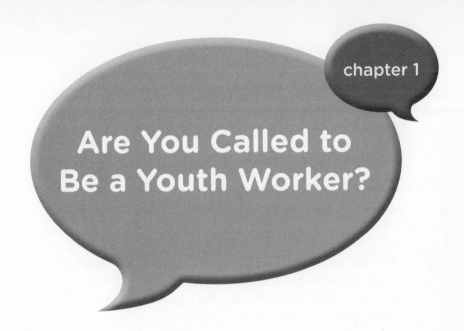

chapter 1

# Are You Called to Be a Youth Worker?

## determine your call to youth ministry

Before you can truly start thinking about the process of starting in a new or existing youth ministry, you should first ask yourself the series of questions I outline below.

There are two ways to approach these questions: 1) You can simply glance over them and come up with off-the-cuff responses; or 2) You can sit down and spend a good amount of time mulling them over, praying about each one. (Hint: You should definitely go with the latter option.)

There's nothing magical about this particular list of questions, but they'll prompt you to identify some things about yourself as the vessel the Holy Spirit will use to work in the lives of teenagers. Knowing how God made you is key to knowing how you'll function best in a youth ministry capacity. Frequently we approach youth ministry with the idea that we have to be like another "successful" youth worker we know. Instead of this approach, focus on how God has created and gifted you for ministry and take some time to think through what that might look like.

### Passion
- What do you get excited about?
- What drives you?

## Personality
- What are you good at?
- What are you bad at?
- What ticks you off? What are your pet peeves?
- Who in ministry do you look up to?
- What kind of ministry are you attracted to?

## Spirituality
- What is God doing in your life? What is he teaching you?
- What are your spiritual gifts?

## Vision
- Where is God leading you spiritually?
- What picture is God painting in your heart for what he wants the ministry to look like?
- What effect do you hope your involvement in youth ministry could have five years from now?

## Experience
- Are you plugged into ministry right now?
- What past experiences do you have in ministry?
- What do others who have seen you work in ministry say?

## Philosophy
- What is your definition of ministry?
- How will you determine if your involvement in youth ministry is successful or not?
- Do you see ministry as a lifestyle or a job? Why?
- If you feel called to vocational youth ministry, what leads you to believe that?

All believers are called to ministry, but few are called to full-time vocational ministry. Some may think that being a youth worker seems like an appealing profession because it looks fun and easy. Or maybe it appears to be a convenient job to transition into after college while figuring out what really lies ahead. More often than not, the people who think that way quit their jobs in frustration, because they didn't take the time to learn more about themselves and how their unique puzzle piece fits into God's big picture, whether that's in youth ministry or elsewhere.

## Other Voices

**Paul Martin:**

That's an awesome list. It looks like something that could also help volunteers determine how they'd like to be involved in youth ministry.

**Mike Kupferer:**

At some point in your ministry, you'll answer these or similar questions. Down the road, usually after a particularly difficult season of ministry, you'll ask yourself if staying in youth ministry is what you want to do. My advice is to answer these questions up front—this will help lay the foundation of your ministry. As I've gone through difficult times, I've found it easier to survive when I've already answered these questions and I know youth ministry is the right, if not always easy, place for me.

**Aaron Giesler:**

It's always a good idea to bring in others on this type of decision. Proverbs 15:22 says, "Plans fail for lack of counsel, but with many advisers they succeed." Good counsel can give you an outside perspective on your strengths and weaknesses. Don't just ask one person—ask several people who know you in different contexts to find out if what you see in yourself is what others see in you.

# three qualities every youth worker must have

In Matthew 25:14–30 Jesus tells a story of three servants, commonly referred to as the parable of the talents. Each of the three servants was in a position to serve his master by overseeing resources that were entrusted to him, "each according to his ability" (verse 15). Two of them were faithful and served their master with great passion. These two were also fruitful, and the resources that were entrusted to them were doubled as a result of their faithful service to their master. They enjoyed their work, and the master rewarded them for it.

However, the third servant wasn't faithful or fruitful, and he didn't enjoy his responsibility. Matthew 25:24–25 indicates that he made excuses for how he managed the resources and that he was ultimately afraid of his master. Because he was neither faithful nor fruitful, the responsibility was taken away from him.

As you evaluate your calling to ministry, consider the following:

- Are you faithful? Can you serve every day with passion?
- Are you fruitful? Are you seeing positive outcomes? Is God blessing your service?
- Are you fulfilled? Do you enjoy ministry? Does it satisfy your heart in a way nothing else can?

All three of these qualities need to be true for you as you head into vocational youth ministry. As you look back over your past experiences in ministry, either volunteer or paid, think about whether or not youth ministry is something you can passionately do every day for as long as your Master calls you to manage his resources. Can you persevere even when the political structure of your church becomes overbearing? Even when a teen criticizes your motives for serving him? Even when it's stressful and taxing on your emotions?

Also consider how you've seen the Lord use you and the fruit of what you've seen take place as a result of your investment in others. When you teach, are there glimpses of life-change and conviction taking place? When you're up late on the phone talking with the teen whose dad just walked out, is she turning to the Lord through your support?

Finally, does youth ministry sound like something that would fulfill you in a way that nothing else could? Or could you just as easily see yourself working a different job or serving in a different area of ministry?

If you're reading this and you're still investigating whether youth ministry is where God is calling you, I encourage you to do two things: First, start volunteering with the teenagers at your local church. It's more difficult to answer these questions when you have no frame of reference on which to base them. And second, find a trusted friend who can walk through some of these questions with you and give you an objective perspective. Sometimes others can see our strengths and weaknesses better than we can.

## Other Voices

### Len Evans:
Charles Spurgeon's advice to his students was, "Do not enter the ministry if you can help it." In other words, if you can be content doing anything else, do something else and live for God's glory in any another vocation. I've shared that advice with five friends over

the last year and only one is still pursuing vocational ministry. I think that's a good percentage. Youth pastors aren't the special forces of ministry but it's too hard to stay in unless you know God pulled you into it.

**Ryan Nielsen:**

One of the important things to remember is what it means to serve passionately. I think too often youth workers take that to mean that every day of the job should be joyful, but that's not the case. I think that serving passionately means remembering who we're doing this for: not the church, not the teens, not the parents, not our family, not even ourselves—we're doing this for God. If he's truly called us to this work, then he'll enable us to serve with a passion for him and his calling on our lives regardless of what challenges we face at our churches or in our youth ministries.

**Tony Myles:**

I'm going to wrestle with these thoughts a bit. I like the intention of them, but if we misunderstand them we may quit our ministry for the wrong reasons. Sometimes in serving we don't feel fulfilled by what we do for God (like Jeremiah, for instance, who wrote Lamentations for a reason). There are also seasons when no matter how hard we try there's nothing on the surface that seems fruitful.

That's why being faithful is really the linchpin in all of this. I'm not implying blind faithfulness to a church or ministry, but instead being faithful to the One who has called you to do something critical with him and for him. Don't just "hang in there," instead, hang onto him. If you do, the fruitfulness and the fulfillment will come—because they'll start in your heart first.

**Lars Rood:**

Loving teens and loving God are still the two first things I look at when talking to people who work with teenagers. I think faithful, fruitful, and fulfilled are pretty good secondary categories. We'll always be in situations where we're called to be faithful in spite of how things are going. We will fail and teens will fail. In my mind, the most important people in youth ministry are those who say, "I commit" and stick to it day in and day out.

## the ideal youth ministry

The ideal youth ministry starts with us, the leaders. The ideal youth pastor isn't the person who can complete the longest bullet point list of tasks—it's the person who knows who she is in ministry and lets everything else flow from that.

For this person, everything stems from two things: love and passion. The ideal youth pastor—

- Passionately loves God. She's devoted to studying Scripture for herself. She's committed to praying constantly, worshiping, and sharing God with others.
- Passionately loves her family. She places her family before ministry and invests more time in them than in any other people.
- Passionately loves teenagers. A given, yes, but not to be taken for granted.
- Passionately loves free time. She regularly takes time off from ministry to relax and reenergize, and she doesn't feel bad about it!
- Passionately leaves a legacy. She knows people are watching her and she lives a contagiously godly example.
- Passionately leads the ministry. She sets the tone and vision for the ministry and remembers that before she's to be a friend for teenagers, she's to be a leader.

If you can be that person and let ministry flow from who you are, you'll do exactly what your ministry needs.

## Other Voices

### Bill Allison:

Where does intentionally training (teens and volunteers) and multiplying our love and passion through them fit into your description of an ideal youth pastor? How many times have we seen a youth pastor move on to another position or ministry—and though he may be remembered for love and passion, the youth ministry left behind limps along for a while and folds up shop . . . until the next youth pastor comes? Can a youth pastor be considered "ideal" without training successors? Should this training and equipping teens and volunteers be a part of the DNA of who a youth pastor is?

### Tim's reply to Bill:

Training is definitely important for a youth ministry leader. I mention it in chapter 11 in #9 of the "10 Commandments for youth workers." I see it as a function that flows out of the passion for leading the ministry.

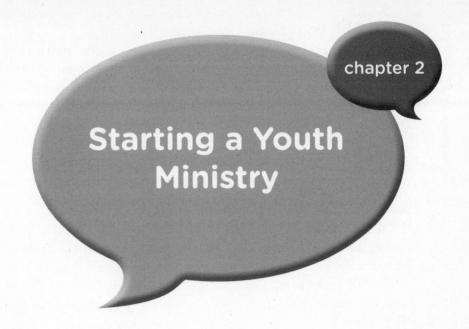

# chapter 2

# Starting a Youth Ministry

## tips for starting out in vocational youth ministry

### 1. Pray.

You can't serve the Lord without regularly talking with him about it. Pray for wisdom, guidance, and vision. Pray for teens, yourself, your family, and those you serve. Saturate the ministry in prayer. Get others to pray for your ministry, too. You can't have a successful ministry without the Lord's involvement. Period.

### 2. Study God's Word.

Youth group isn't just a place to teach Scripture to others, it's one of the few jobs in the world where you actually get paid to study the Bible. How cool is that? As a leader, you can't take people to a place you've never been yourself, so make sure you're continuing to grow before taking the responsibility to help others grow.

### 3. Set boundaries.

Say things like, "No," and, "It's time for you all to go home." The natural tendency is to become over-involved at the very beginning because you're excited to be there and to change lives for Christ. Having this passion is great, but don't let it set a workload precedence you can't sustain over a period of time. Remember, it's better to do a few things well than many poorly.

## 4. Talk with your supervisor regularly.

Whether that be your senior pastor or someone else, make sure you're communicating often—both when things are going well and when they're not. I recommend that you meet once a week to talk about what's going on in the youth ministry and how you can work together as a team. This helps create accountability and builds trust. And believe me, you can never have too much trust built when tough times strike.

## 5. Invest in volunteers.

If you don't have adult youth workers yet, get some. (See chapter 6.) Even if your group consists of only one teen, you need help. If you already have a team of youth leaders in place, invest in them like crazy. Train them, build relationships with them, and include them in all your plans. Without them you'll make a lot of dumb decisions. Plus, see number 3—you shouldn't attempt to do everything yourself.

## 6. Spend time with teens, not your office.

The temptation is to get the youth ministry organized and all the programming straightened out. But—especially at the beginning—teens don't care what you do in the office all day. They have a brand-new youth pastor and they want to know who you are and whether or not you'll care for them well more than they want to know whether you have great organizational skills. Invite them over to your house or apartment (with other adults present, of course), go to their sports games and concerts, go out to eat after school, and make yourself available online.

## 7. Don't change everything right away.

Every youth pastor has his own unique style, giftedness, passion, and talents—so every youth ministry will be different. It is important that you mold the ministry according to how God has created you, but don't do it all right away. Take at least a year to get to know the people and the ministry before making any major changes. Once you've built trust and taken time to learn how the church functions, you'll have much more support to make those big changes without forcing people to turn their back on what they've known.

## 8. Keep your motives in check.

There's a lot of pressure to start a new youth ministry position with a bang. Expectations are high—regardless of whether they're self-inflicted or from the church. It's important that you keep your motives in check and remember why you're in ministry in the first place. Don't plan something big just to impress people. Never do ministry to please people. Ministry is always about pleasing and serving God.

## 9. Be transparent.

No one knows everything, and no one can have extensive experience for every situation. Admit your weaknesses. Be honest when you're not sure how to handle a situation. You may fear that transparency will erode authority and respect, but actually the exact opposite will happen. It's okay if you don't have all the answers. Trying to know everything isn't key—knowing where to find the answers is. Again, that's why you surround yourself with a team of other youth workers.

## 10. Stay in shape.

Not just because it's fun to keep up with the teens in dodgeball, but because it reduces stress, gives you more energy, and helps you stay alert. Seriously, the difference exercise makes in ministry is unbelievable. Sure it requires discipline for most of us, but using discipline is just as healthy as exercise. If for no other reason, stay in shape in order to be a good steward of your body, which is a temple of the Holy Spirit.

## Other Voices

### Steve Blanchard:

I would like to add to #4: I had a pastor once say, "Every church has a church boss." These are the people in the church who have the power to defend or hurt your ministry. Figure out who the influencers are in your specific ministry and in the church itself and do what it takes to create trust with them. Win these people over.

### Jeff Graham:

In addition to #3 I'd add that it's important to stay focused on the area(s) you were hired to do. Shortly after I arrived at my church, someone informed me that there were no paper towels in the men's bathroom. Luckily, I didn't know where the paper towels were stored (otherwise I would have changed them myself). Instead I directed them to one of our janitors. Youth pastors need to be able to focus on the job of caring for teens.

**Brian Kirk:**

I'd like to echo #7. I've known pastors and youth pastors who felt the need to start making changes right away—big changes that ended with them losing their position before six months was up. There's great wisdom in picking your battles your first year or two at the church—make changes necessary for the health of the ministry, but otherwise follow the maxim: year one—learn them, year two(love them, year three—lead them.

**Justin Ross:**

For the first year or so, write a weekly report and put it into a three-ring notebook. Nothing long and extravagant—just a few paragraphs. Write about the youth ministry: stories of great things that are happening and things you're planning and envisioning for the future. This does a couple of things. First, it helps you look back and see how you are progressing. Second, it gives you some protection if someone in the church wants to challenge what you've been up to for the past few months. You can just smile and say, "Let me show you."

## why teens come to youth group

Before we start a youth ministry, it's important to know why teens come to youth group in the first place. Do they come to learn? To have a good time? To worship? To avoid homework? To get out of the house?

We'd like to believe that teens come to our youth ministries to hear powerful teaching, to grow spiritually, and to become disciples who devote their lives to worship and to spreading the gospel. Although those reasons may be true for some students, those teens are probably in the minority.

In my experience, teenagers come to youth group primarily because of the relationships. The reverse of this is also true: Students who aren't connected in meaningful relationships in the youth ministry don't care to be there.

So as we get started in youth ministry, why do we spend most of our time planning events and programs? Often the greatest impact we can have is just by showing teens that we love them and that God does, too. Youth group doesn't need to launch with cool stuff, big games, amazing events, or even dynamic teachers. We sometimes think teens need a smorgasbord of activities to choose from, and that having teenagers involved in programs means they must be growing spiritually. But, in fact, the opposite is often true. Having a large number of teens involved in youth group doesn't necessarily mean they're growing spiritually—it just means we're keeping them busy. And busyness usually hinders spiritual growth because it distracts us from the personal time we need to spend with our Creator. In fact, in the church world it's very easy for teens (and adults, too) to start substituting church activities for a personal relationship with Christ. That's when teens answer the question, "Are you a Christian?" with something like, "Yes, I go to church twice a week."

Now, programs aren't necessarily bad. Just use them to enhance your spiritually influential relationships in order to take teens deep into God's Word and wide with his message to the world. Remember that programs are a tool—plan and implement them purposely. Your time with teenagers is too short to spend it running programs just for the sake of having a youth program or because it sounded like something "cool" to do.

Often our priorities are backward. The old cliché really is true: People don't care how much you know until they know how much you care. And—though it may seem counterintuitive—the best way you can show teens you care is by making sure your relationship with them is not your primary relationship.

Your own relationship with Christ should come first. How can you model mature Christian faith if you're not growing? Teens need to see the priority of your relationship with Christ as something real and genuine—not just something you talk about. Plus, the more your love grows for the Lord, the more your love will grow for the teens around you.

Your second priority is your relationship with your family. Teens need to see a positive family dynamic modeled—especially when many of them have no idea what a healthy family should look like. Also, without the support of your family, the ministry will eventually crumble. But more importantly, your spouse and your children need to know that they're more important to you than youth group.

Your third priority should be relationships with teens and parents. When God and your family are in their respective places in your life, your relational ministry to teenagers and their families will be more effective as you become the role model they need.

## Other Voices

**Franklin Wood:**

What Tim says about relational ministry is so true, but it's hard to break yourself of this kind of thinking if you're in the habit of program-driven youth ministry.

What I've done this year is to write "pray" at the beginning of every day in my day planner. I know this sounds terrible, but it's a reminder to me of what's important. At about 3:30 p.m. I've written, "call teens," and I schedule nothing past this point.

I also printed up one page per teen with one column labeled date and the other labeled topics discussed. This is so I can check records to keep myself accountable. I want to make sure I'm trying to call all the teens and not playing favorites. I also want to keep track of what's going on in their lives so that the next time I call, I can ask about our previous discussion.

It's worked pretty well so far, but I'm still struggling.

We've really messed up when it comes to being there for teens. Simple things like calling people and showing up for a visit go a long way.

# 10 steps to starting a youth ministry in your church

Your church might want to offer a youth ministry program just because "that's what real churches do these days" or because members want to have activities available for their teenagers. And you could start a youth ministry just by organizing a program and hoping teens connect to it, but your ministry will be left with little vision or direction.

Here's a very basic structure of how a church might go about starting a youth ministry that will have a bit more direction and focus:

## 1. Pray.

Fervently ask the Lord to guide the entire process—to provide the necessary ideas and thoughts to make it all happen for his glory.

## 2. Put together a small core team.

Your team should be comprised of teens, parents, and volunteers who believe in teenagers and have a heart for reaching them for Christ. Gather and pray for wisdom and guidance for this new ministry.

## 3. Develop a vision and direction with this core team.

Answer some of these questions together:

- Why are we starting this group?
- Who do we intend to reach?
- Where do we want to be this time next year? In five years?
- What kind of atmosphere do we intend to create for the students relationally and spiritually? What core values will drive everything we do in this ministry? (This includes how we spend our time, where we invest resources, what we teach, and what programs we run.)
- What is each of us most passionate about in ministry?

## 4. Based on your answers, formulate a strategy for accomplishing these things.

How are you going to get to where God has called you to be? For example, if your group is led to minister to unchurched students at a particular high school, how are you going to connect with these teens in order to address both their felt and actual needs? What environment will allow you to teach and reach those teenagers most effectively?

## 5. Communicate your strategy.

Once your strategy is clear, written down, and understood by all those on the core team, share it with the church leadership. Make any necessary revisions.

## 6. Assign roles and responsibilities to each of the team members.

Assign roles and responsibilities to all who are involved in fulfilling the strategy. Determine launch dates for each aspect of the ministry. Give yourself the freedom to launch in only one or two areas and build from there as the group solidifies.

## 7. Share your values and strategy with the church body.

Make sure you speak to the church as a whole before you launch your youth ministry. There may be some people in the congregation who have contradictory opinions and values, but that's all right. Just listen to what they have to say, respect their opinions and let them know you value their input. There'll be many more who're excited and will support you 100 percent.

## 8. Prayerfully launch the ministry.

Continue to drench the ministry in prayer as you kick off your first youth group meetings. Recruit other adult leaders as necessary and get them on board with your group's vision and strategy. Teach them to continually pray for the youth ministry, too.

## 9. After six months or so, reevaluate.

Take a look at your values, goals, and strategies; and then make whatever tweaks are necessary:

- What's been working well that should continue?
- What isn't serving its purpose and needs to be cut?
- How is the ministry progressing in the direction you set, and what are the next steps for taking it where it still needs to go?

## 10. Implement any necessary changes and proceed accordingly.

After you've spent some time reevaluating, pray and determine where the Lord is leading. Then start communicating about the changes you plan to make in the ministry. Once you've shared your plans with the church's senior pastor, teens, families, and anyone else who needs to know; start implementing what you've discussed.

Remember to pray, pray, and pray harder. The only way your ministry will succeed is if you're saturated in prayer and if you constantly follow the Lord's direction for his ministry. He desires to see teenagers come to know him and grow in their faith even more than you desire it. Pray and listen for him to tell you where he's leading.

### Other Voices

**Jason Curlee:**

Here's my thought on #3: Because the student ministry will be a part of the much larger church, a vision for it has already been established. There should only be one vision: that of the church. One of the roles of a student ministry is to help fulfill that vision. My advice would be to develop a mission and strategy that leads the student ministry in fulfilling the vision of the church.

**Glenn W. Davies:**

Don't fall into the trap of "maintaining" a program or merely creating a fun club for your teens. It's shallow and temporary, and it lacks true purpose and depth. There's enough entertainment out there and most teenagers are overstimulated already. Give them some real substance!

Here are a few tips that I pray will encourage some of you out there:

- Get teens hungry for God! Teens love to eat. This is true physically, but it's also true spiritually. Get them hungry for the Word, and each week let them chow down on just enough so they leave wanting more.
- Pray with your teens and have them pray with and for each other. Make it a priority each week. Pretty soon your prayer time will become the most precious part of your evenings together.
- Put your youth group out where your congregation can see them—let the adults know what God's doing. Help them be witnesses of God's love in your town, neighborhood, or community.
- Give your teens ownership of their group and involve everybody in order to nurture a sense of belonging and value.
- More than anything, remember that it's God's ministry, not yours. Give him all the praise and glory!

## but what if my church has only one teenager?

Some time ago a mother from a very small town in Kentucky shared with me that she and her family are attending a church where her daughter is the only teenager in the entire church. Being the dedicated mom she is, she tried everything she could think of to get other teens into their church—she even talked to the church about the possibility of hiring a part-time youth pastor in order to draw teens in. Frustrated, she said, "We do a family devotion each night at home, but I think having other adults help with her Christian education is a good idea. How do we get a youth ministry started with only one teenager?"

Youth ministry is valuable and it's honorable to strive to start one in your church; however, there's nothing wrong with not having a youth group. Many parents have raised their teenagers quite well without the influence of a church youth ministry. Be prayerful and discerning and consider the possibility that your church may not need a youth group. If this is the case, don't force it. Instead, try to utilize any adult/teen relationships that happen outside of a youth group context. If the one or two teens in your church have one or two adults they seem to enjoy and respect at church, ask those people if they'd be interested in spending time with those teens outside of church.

That's how I got kick-started in youth ministry in the first place. My story is very similar to that of this woman's daughter, except that I had two brothers who were close to me in age. The three of us were often the only teenagers in our Sunday school class. An adult from a local high school campus ministry started meeting with me for lunch and picking me up to tag along as he ran errands and attended meetings, and eventually his passion for God's Word and his enthusiasm for sharing his faith with teens became contagious. It's because of that relationship that I'm in youth ministry today—not because I grew up in a dynamic youth group at a big church somewhere.

If your teen doesn't seem to naturally connect with any of the adults in the church, pick a few godly adults and speak with them about investing in the teen. If the teenager is a girl, maybe start by suggesting a girls' night out where the ladies of the church go do something fun together. Encourage the ladies to invite the teen along. If the teen is a boy, see if any of the men of the church would be willing to take him out with the guys.

Also, if you're involved in an adult Bible study, invite the teenager to that. There's great value for a teenager in being surrounded by a host of spiritual adults who can mentor, advise, and guide her through these formative years.

Furthermore, find unique ways the teen can serve the body as the only teenager in the church. It'll teach her that youth ministry is not just about what the church does for her, but also that youth ministry is about teens ministering.

Essentially, forget the youth ministry thing and bring the teen into the adult ministries where those adults can eventually become the "youth ministry" for that teen.

## Other Voices

**Brian Eberly:**
I completely agree. Healthy relationships with godly adults are far more important than cool activities. I might also add, find ways for teens to serve within the overall life of the church. They need to feel as much ownership in the church as the adults do.

**David Schmoyer:**

I'm Tim's brother, and I went to the same youth group he did. During that time (7th-9th grade) the person who made the biggest impact on my life was a Christian man in our church named Norman Greb. Mr. Greb would often invite my brothers and me to work with him doing light construction throughout the year. We worked hard, ate lunch together, and talked. There was no pressure to bond, and there were no forced meetings. Mr. Greb impacted my life by allowing me to be around him and to watch his life. This taught me far more about godly manhood than I remember from youth group.

## how to grow a youth group

It's really not that complicated. It requires four things:

1. Be passionate about your own personal relationship with Christ.
2. Develop and train volunteers who are also passionate about their relationship with Christ.
3. Hang out with teenagers, and as you intentionally mention God in your conversations, pray that your passion becomes contagious.
4. Expect the Holy Spirit to do some awesome things to spiritually grow your teens.

(What, did you think this was about numerical growth? Are you a little disappointed that it's not?)

The first point is this: It starts with us, the youth leaders. In order to take our teens to new levels of spiritual maturity we must be at that level first. We can stand up in front of a group and say a lot of meaningful things about God, and although that's an important part of ministry, none of that will have the same impact as the presence of a passionate, sold-out-for-God youth worker. Someone who's in love with God will give teens a chance to see a relationship with God lived out in daily life.

The second point is that spiritual growth is ultimately a work of the Holy Spirit. There's nothing we can do to force a teenager to grow. The best we can do is pray like their lives depend on it (because they do) and seek the Lord's wisdom in creating environments that facilitate spiritual growth. Beyond that, the best we can do is remain open for the Lord to use us to communicate his truth and then stand back and let him be the one who makes the truth penetrate the hearts and souls of our teens.

## Other Voices

### Jason Curlee:

Curious . . . what's wrong with numerical growth? What's wrong with wanting to reach out to impact many lives and teaching our teens to do the same?

I want numbers because I want lives impacted and changed, instead of on track to a path that leads away from God. Maybe it comes down to terminology. I also want to be faithful to those teens and help each of them grow to be full disciples of Christ and then teach them to reach out to their generation. I guess I'm also no longer afraid of saying I'm about numbers. I'm about numbers of teens and adults no longer going down a path of death and destruction.

I also think that it's really the heart of people who want to make true impact. If it's only numbers for the satisfaction of having large numbers then yes, that's wrong. If it's numbers for the sake of Christ impact, then that's okay.

### Tim's reply to Jason:

I get what you're saying, and I agree with you. I like how Perry Noble (via Rick Warren in *The Purpose Driven Church* [1995]) puts it, "Numbers matter because numbers represent souls!" But for too many people (although they'll never openly admit it), numbers are the primary focus. People tend to get excited about material that shows them how to grow a larger ministry because that's success that can be easily measured and will provide a sense of accomplishment. It's almost impossible to measure and quantify spiritual growth, and in our American culture—which places so much emphasis on accomplishments and checking off to-do lists—that just doesn't sit as well. I think we'd all agree that growing toward Christlikeness is the most important thing, but there's nothing wrong with having a large ministry with lots of people, either. And just because a ministry is large doesn't mean that it's more effective than a smaller ministry down the street.

### Mike Kupferer:

I agree with Tim that the focus should not be on numerical growth, but rather on spiritual growth. I believe that having a large number of teens who abandon their faith during or after college will do more harm to the church than any perceived benefit of having large numbers. If you're keeping track of numbers in order to gauge the spiritual status of your teens, you might be missing the point, too. I'd rather have an adult purposely shepherding a few students, because that person would notice that Johnny hasn't been to Bible study lately. It might be a small difference, but I believe this personal touch is more effective than looking at anonymous numbers to tell the health of a ministry.

**Justin Ross:**

I've been at my current church for nine years and in that time only one person has challenged me for not having a large enough youth group. My response to him was not one I recommend, but it did illustrate the point. I told him we'd have hundreds of teenagers next week—I just needed him to buy the pizza and beer kegs.

Honestly, anyone can draw a crowd. We've done it for years in youth ministry with huge outreach events. Many seasoned youth pastors will agree that these events do draw teens—but many are from other youth groups who drop by to participate in the fun, and the ministry sees little, if any, numerical growth from them.

Turn any questions about numbers into conversations about health. What makes your group a healthy one? Healthy youth groups are growing youth groups (in more ways than one).

# what to do during your first youth group meeting

So you're starting at your youth ministry position, and your first official meeting with the teenagers is less than a week away. What should you do that first night? Should you focus totally on relationships and creating a positive first impression? Should you dive right into an in-depth Bible study to take advantage of the undivided attention you'll have?

Although the latter aspiration is admirable, it's best that you don't start a deep Bible study series on the first night. On that first night, no one is thinking, "I wonder how well this guy can teach the Bible?" Instead, everyone is thinking, "Who is this guy, and why should I listen to him?"

Take that first evening to introduce yourself. Share about your teenage years, your family, how you came to know Christ, what God has been teaching you lately, your hobbies, interests, etc. Also come prepared to ask them questions—especially if it's a smaller group. Have the teenagers share a little bit about themselves, and give each teen special attention as he speaks. While they share, show interest by asking follow-up questions. For example, if a teen says he likes to read, ask what books he's recently read. Or, if he's on a sports team right now, ask him how the team is doing this year.

Basically, you'll be establishing a lot of first impressions that first night. Don't be paranoid about it—just be yourself while being intentional about what first impressions you leave. You want teens to sense that you're a real person and that you're someone they can relate to—someone who cares about each of them.

## Other Voices

### Roy Probus:

I always spend the first youth group night talking about myself. I share my testimony and what God has put on my heart for the new youth group—nothing major, I keep it light. I've found that this is a great way to do it, especially if you have parents in the group or others who haven't had a chance to meet you yet.

### Aaron Giesler:

If a person gives his testimony at a youth group meeting, it can—and should—be a great lesson from Scripture (original sin, sin, propitiation, repentance, justification, etc. . . . )

### Jeff Wright:

I've got to weigh in and ask how anyone could question the fact that the most important thing any minister does in any setting is proclaim the Word.

Don't get me wrong. Relationships are great. They can model and reinforce the truths taught in teaching. But again, if one had to choose between the two, the only legitimate option is giving the priority to preaching.

### Tim's response to Jeff:

Those of you who separate the relationship part from scriptural teaching are probably approaching ministry from your perspective, rather than a teenager's perspective. Maybe a relationship wouldn't make a big difference to you, but it's absolutely essential to teenagers. That's not to deny that a sermon from someone they've never heard won't make an impact, because it certainly can. It's just that teens listen more intently to you when they know that you love them.

**Justin Ross:**

Often we try to make our youth group just like our Sunday morning church services. One of our goals should be to plug teens into the ministry and mission of our congregation. Why do we lose so many teens when they graduate? Often, they've spent six to seven years as part of a youth group and when the youth group is not there anymore, they fall away. Sure, preaching is important—so important that the Sunday morning sermon is just as much for teens as it is for adults. What's missing from Sunday morning worship? The opportunity to build relationships. So this is where I begin. There's still a place for preaching in youth ministry, but if you build relationships, those relationships will lead to fantastic Bible study and growth in ministry.

At your first meeting, serve root beer floats (or hot chocolate in the winter), play some get-to-know-you games, and spend time dreaming together. Roll out a huge piece of butcher paper, divide it into sections important to your ministry, and begin throwing out ideas: ideas for missions, ministry, fun days, games, retreats . . . whatever you can come up with. Then have the teens sign the paper. Return to these ideas (and add to them) every so often. Let this represent the dreams, goals, and vision of the ministry.

## after the very first youth group meeting

After that first youth group meeting is over, continue to keep it light and fun for the next few weeks. Focus on building relationships with the teens, learning their names, and familiarizing yourself with the group's atmosphere.

Ask some of the parents to provide snacks and drinks. Teens may feel more comfortable if they have a natural distraction that allows them to do something besides maintaining eye contact throughout a conversation.

Come to each meeting prepared with games, icebreakers, and personal stories. I learned the hard way that it's usually better to over-prepare, just in case something doesn't work out as well as you anticipate. It's awkward to see games that you think are fun flop badly, and if that game is the only activity you've planned, then you have nothing to do for the next hour. If the meeting flies by and you still have a lot on your list of activities for the evening, you can always save your material for the next week.

For those first several weeks—and even months—there are a few main questions likely going through the teenagers' minds:

1. Can I trust this person?
2. Does this person care about me?
3. Who is this person and what is he all about?
4. What's going to happen with our youth group now, and will I like what happens?

The first two are infinitely more important than the third and fourth. If they trust you and know that you love them, you could almost do anything to the youth ministry and still have their support. (It doesn't quite work the same way with parents and church leadership, though!)

The best way to build trust is to model vulnerability and let them see that you're a real person who's not afraid to be open and authentic. If they see that you can be that way, they'll feel safer doing the same with you and will naturally be more trusting. That doesn't mean you should tell them all your deep dark secrets—on the contrary! There are many things that are inappropriate for students to know. But you can easily share about trials, disappointments, successes, victories, and heartache.

## Other Voices

### Benjer McVeigh:

Building trust will be very important as you begin, and appropriate vulnerability is a must. If you're succeeding another youth minister at the church, it might become even more important, because the students will probably miss the former youth minister and might have an attitude of "you'll never replace [youth minister's name]." The good news is that you can't do that, nor is it your job to replace him. Feel free to acknowledge what has come before and praise the good things that have been going on (don't criticize things you may not agree with). Once the teens understand that you aren't there to replace what has come before, but that instead you'll build on the positive, they'll be more open to you.

## Note

If you haven't ever read anything on boundaries, check out *Boundaries: When to Say Yes, When to Say No to Take Control of Your Life* (1992) by Dr. Henry Cloud and Dr. John Townsend.

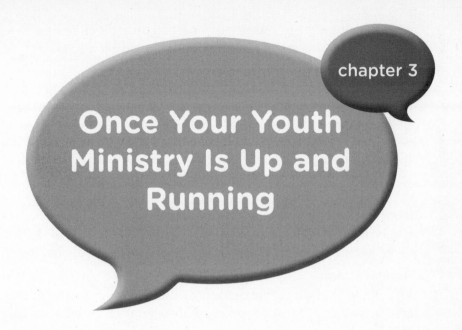

# chapter 3

# Once Your Youth Ministry Is Up and Running

## where real ministry takes place

Life-changing ministry isn't about sitting in a church office planning events and games. It's not about the next big trip, how many teens are in attendance, or how much money is in the budget. Although these things have their obvious place, life-changing ministry usually takes place in those seemingly insignificant moments we soon forget. You're reminded of how important these moments are when you receive the unexpected text message from a teen that says, "Hey, remember last year when you and I were just standing around talking and you said such-and-such? That changed my life forever." Or the random Facebook message that says, "You probably don't remember me, but I was scared and lonely and you gave me a hug. I'm alive today because I felt like you actually cared." Or the phone rings and the voice on the other line says, "I just wanted to let you know that I'm now a church worship leader because of your influence on me during high school. Thank you." Wow.

Here I am today, writing this book, and I'm no different. I'm in youth ministry because of a Student Venture staff member named Bob Klein who invested in me in such a way that his contagious passion for teenagers rubbed off. Several years ago I had the opportunity to take him out to lunch, just as he did for me in high school and say, "Bob, thanks for your influence on my life. Here's where I am today because of it."

Youth ministry isn't only about what you do in the church office—it's about who you are in everyday life to the people you serve.

## Other Voices

### Shan Smith:

This point is made clear to me each week when I go into the local schools to build relationships and share the gospel with students. In the small amount of time I invest outside the walls of my office, I see students who wouldn't (or aren't allowed to) walk through the doors of our local churches being transformed by Christ. With a weekly attendance at one local middle school of 225 students who gather for a donut, devotional, and prayer before school, I have come to believe that real ministry happens outside the church.

### Aaron Giesler:

One of the frustrating things about working with teens is that they are "in process." I have worked with several teens who seemed to have the perfect gifts for an incredible ministry, but left the faith after graduation. On the other hand, there are teens who only occasionally came to youth group who have now become vocational youth workers. Working with teens means you have to trust that God is able to finish what he starts in the lives of our teens. You only get them for a little while, so make the best use of your time with them.

# how to do youth ministry all wrong

Despite knowing better, the way I actually lead my church's youth ministry is often from the mentality that our youth ministry is a program or service we provide to families. I unintentionally feed the consumer perspective by saying things such as, "We offer small groups . . ." and, "We provide connection points for your teens . . ." I'm not convinced that youth ministry is supposed to be about what a paid staff member and a couple of adult volunteers are expected to spiritually provide for teens and families.

Youth ministry shouldn't be about how the church can serve the youth or even how we can provide programs that help them grow spiritually—that's the parents' responsibility. In fact, the youth ministry should be careful not to enable parents to outsource their God-given responsibility to us—something I know my ministry is guilty of. Support parents, yes. Enable them to hand over responsibility for their teens' spiritual lives? No.

The Greek word for church is ekklesia, which means "called out ones." Church is a community of believers who are "called out" from the world to serve and edify each other and the people around them.

Instead of fueling the consumer mentality of what a church offers or provides and which church in town does it best, youth ministry should be about helping teens use their God-given gifts to serve the body. It should teach families that youth ministry isn't just about what the church does for them, but that they are called out to think beyond themselves with a servant's heart. I wonder if the number of teens who leave the church after high school would decrease if teens actually served as an essential part of the local body of Christ, both inside the church and outside of it in the community.

Youth ministry should be less about us doing youth ministry and more about youth doing ministry.

I've known this for a long time, but it's just now starting to really sink in for me. It demands a pretty radical shift, one that will take vision and courage to carry out.

Our programs program people to consume from the church, and I'm programmed to run programs.

Please note, I'm not necessarily anti-program—it's just that we often end up serving the programs instead of using them as very dispensable tools that will equip teen believers to serve the body of Christ.

This could be a healthy discussion to have with the rest of your youth ministry team or even your church staff. Should youth ministry be more about providing a service or creating servants? What if focusing on the latter causes all those with the consumer mentality of the former to leave the group? Is it okay for your youth group to shrink numerically if it's for the right reasons?

## Other Voices

### Steve Cullum:

Even though I don't always do this, I have always tried to keep the mindset that youth ministry (like all ministries) is built on relationships. It's up to our adults to cultivate relationships with our teens and their parents in order to do two things: build up the family structure in order to allow families to honor God together, and be the family for the teens who don't have godly parents. All the other stuff in youth ministry should cultivate those relationships. Our goal is to love teens and families as Christ has loved us. We just happen to use programs as one tool.

### Troy Young:

We can look at the church as one body with many parts (1 Corinthians 12:20). I believe we need to look at student ministry as a smaller part of the main body, all working together to fulfill one purpose, and that is to glorify Jesus Christ.

Oftentimes—and I'm very guilty of this—we try to make ourselves look and act differently than the main body. We give ourselves a different name, a different logo, a different purpose statement, and a different teaching method from the main body. I think this is wrong, and I think it's one of the reasons graduates drop out of church.

This is where I'm starting to change. I'm making the student ministry look as similar to the main body as possible. We use the same logo and the same name, we use the same technique to teach the Word, and our purpose statement says, "Our purpose is to fulfill the purpose of the main body of the church."

I know some of you are saying, "No way—I'll lose everyone if I do that." Well guess what—my youth group is growing—not only numerically, but our current youth ministry is more spiritually solid than it has been in the last 12 years. Many of our graduating seniors from last year have committed to colleges close to the church so they can continue to serve. That is a first for us.

### Corey Potter:

I love the ideas in this post. In fact I think I totally agree. I only have one question: What about the teens whose parents don't mentor, encourage, love, or teach them about Christ? Honestly, the majority of the teens in our youth group have parents who probably never talk to them about God—or anything else for that matter. Our church has offered training for parents, and is willing to teach parents about how to connect with their children, but I see very little evidence of this happening. If the teens aren't getting any spiritual guidance at home, and definitely not at school, where should they get it?

### Tim's response to Corey:

That's part of my tension, too. For some teens, if they don't get it at church, they don't get it anywhere at all.

What I'm thinking, though, isn't that we eliminate spiritual training at church, but rather that we cultivate a value for both the ministry and demonstrate to parents that it's ultimately their responsibility, and that we're here to support them.

Another option could be to have the parents continue to be the spiritual leaders at church and allow the teenagers who don't have Christian parents to sit in with a family that does. This way all the parents essentially become youth leaders.

## lies we believe in youth ministry

### Eh, it's good enough.

You should never look at a Bible lesson, worship set, or even the ministry in general and think that it's up to par. Rather, strive for excellence in all you do and "work at it with all your heart, as working for the Lord, not for human masters, since you know that you will receive an inheritance from the Lord as a reward. It is the Lord Christ you are serving." (Colossians 3:23-24).

### It's not about numbers.

Even though numbers aren't the most important part of youth ministry, numbers are important because they show that you're not an inward-focused Christian bubble. You should be intentionally reaching out in your community and seeking the lost for Christ, because every number out there represents a lost soul.

### I need to pretend I'm perfect so teenagers look up to me.

Actually, teens need to see that you're a human being who makes mistakes, has failures and sometimes struggles in your walk with Christ. It doesn't make you a bad role model—it makes you someone they can actually relate to. Of course, teenagers are not licensed psychiatrists, so make sure you have some healthy boundaries in place. (More on this in chapter 8.)

### We can't do effective youth ministry without a budget, a cool youth room and a paid youth pastor.

There's nothing that suppresses imagination, creativity, and excitement more than focusing on what you don't have. Instead, focus on the tools and resources God has provided and run with that. The best ministry often takes place outside the church, with a free activity and a volunteer youth worker who just loves teens.

### It's wrong and hurtful, but I'll let it go.

Avoiding issues that need to be addressed (gossip, disrespect, etc.) will erode unity faster than anything else. Confront these issues head-on for the sake of the ministry even if it makes you feel uncomfortable.

### I'm not funny or outgoing. I don't play a guitar, have no facial hair, and I'm over 40—there's no way I can work with teens.

The best youth workers I've ever encountered are retired, have white or no hair, know nothing about the latest bands or movies, but deeply love teenagers and have lives that are jam-packed with spiritual maturity and wisdom that no young adult could ever impart.

### We need to play games and have lots of fun at youth group.

Yes, you do need to have fun at youth group, but it doesn't solely have to be through hype and games. Exploring Scripture together can be incredibly fun, too! So can sitting around a coffee table talking about your week or working on some sort of project together.

### This is pointless. I don't see any life-change taking place.

And you may never see it. Sometimes the investment you make now doesn't pay off until years down the road when you may no longer be in touch with the teens. Speak God's truth into the lives of the teens and let the Holy Spirit do the rest.

### We need to have lots of programs and activities for teenagers.

Having a full calendar may actually be a symptom of insecurity more than a sign of strength. Besides, just because teens participate in church events doesn't mean they're actually growing—it just means you're keeping them busy.

### They're just teenagers. I can't expect too much from them.

Teenagers have more potential than any other age group. They're leaders and innovators, they're creative, passionate, and have more energy than 100 youth pastors on energy drinks. They're incredibly responsible about whatever is important to them. Maybe your expectations are too low. Challenge your teens to a higher standard.

## Other Voices

**Shane Yancey:**

I have to disagree. You can't be a youth pastor without facial hair. I shaved my goatee off last month and was almost fired. (I can't think of a good way to make sure people know I'm kidding. Darn you computer and your poor rendering of sarcasm!)

**Ben Bacon:**

I couldn't agree more. As a former youth group(-er? -ee?), I respected the guys who were real with me and taught the Bible. The passion of those men has stayed with me.

# helping teens take ownership of youth group

I know that many youth workers struggle with trying to help their teens take ownership of their youth group. Sometimes it's because it's not clearly understood by the teen or the youth worker what exactly they're taking ownership of. Other times it's because encouraging the teens to "take ownership" is really a fancy way of getting teenagers to do some work.

Most ownership comes naturally to teenagers when they know you (the youth pastor), trust you, and even love you. This means you have to get involved in their lives. Invite teens over for a meal, go to their games and concerts, take them out for pizza after school, and so on. I help coach the high school wrestling team in our community, so during the wrestling season I'm on their campus every day after school.

Here are two examples of how teens have taken ownership in my youth group based on our relationship:

## Story One:

I met with a high school guy every Wednesday after school to go out to eat and have one-on-one discipleship conversation. Because of the relationship we developed, one night at youth group I said, "Hey, here's the game I'm thinking about leading, but I'm not sure if it'll work or not. What do you think?" He told me it was lame and offered a different idea, which was great. So I asked him if he would lead his game idea for us. He agreed and took over and everyone had a lot of fun.

## Story Two:

A girl in my youth group has a heart for people who are less fortunate and is a huge fan of 30 Hour Famine. Rather than me planning the whole thing, she agreed to help with it the first year. But then two years in a row she took charge of the whole thing without me. She just needed to see that she had my support.

I think it works like this:

1. Develop the relationship.
2. Have teenagers join you in ministry.
3. Give them ownership of it.

Jumping to #3 doesn't work.

## Other Voices

**Waldy Schröder:**

What can I do if I have a youth ministry with more than 100 students?

**Tim's reply to Waldy:**

My youth group also has more than 100 students. I obviously can't spend individual time with all of them on a consistent basis, so I team up with other adult leaders. Together we can invest in different teenagers. And even if you don't have enough adult leaders, don't let that stop you from spending time building relationships with a few teens. It's better to invest in a few than in none of them at all.

**Jordan Muck:**

Discipleship and one-on-one growth is key. We are seeing this with our teens as well. We embrace them, give them a chance to run with an activity, and support them whether it's successful or it tanks. No matter the outcome, they're able to experience ownership and leadership.

# five tips for making visitors feel welcome at youth group

## 1. Place signs around the facility so visitors know exactly how to get to the room where your meeting is.

We all feel intimidated when we're in a new place with new people, so it's important that teens can easily find their way around without feeling lost.

## 2. Make sure you talk with visiting teens.

It sounds like a no-brainer, but it's still easily overlooked when there are last-minute preparations to make and other connections you need to make before people go home. The questions going through every visitor's mind are, "Am I accepted here?" and, "Is this a place where I can feel like I belong?" So as soon as a visitor arrives, do your best to answer both of those questions for her with a yes. Just make sure that when you talk to her, you don't only talk about yourself and the ministry (which is easy to do if you're nervous). Instead, talk about her. And whatever you do, don't ask her questions like, "Are you new here?" and "Is this your first time here?" That reminds her that she doesn't fit in quite yet and that she's an outsider. Instead, say things like, "I don't think I've met you yet. I'm Tim. What's your name?"

### 3. Learn names and use them.
The generic, "Hey you, in the red shirt!" won't make a teen feel like this is a place where he's known, accepted, and valued. Using his name will help him know you care.

### 4. Get contact information.
But only ask for what's completely necessary. More and more teens are leery of parting with personal information, especially when they're giving it to a stranger. Sometimes all you need is a first and last name—then ask, "Are you on Facebook?"

### 5. Follow up with the new teens during the week.
Use whatever contact info you got from the new teens and say hi (using their names, of course). Don't try to market your ministry or make a sales pitch about why he should come back. Just say how great it was to meet him and ask if there's any way you can pray for him throughout the week. That communicates that you care about him, not that you just want to add numbers to your youth group.

Most churches think they're welcoming, but all of us have visited a church and decided we weren't going back. Studies show that when a visitor enters your church, many of them have decided within the first two minutes whether they're coming back or not. That's why it's so important to make sure your group is intentional about making positive first impressions—especially if your church claims to be welcoming to outsiders.

## Other Voices

**Nick Arnold:**

One thing that always made me feel welcomed and comfortable in a group was when the youth pastor would ask me to stand up and single me out as a visitor. Just kidding.

**Eric Groezinger:**

To further your second point, I learned a small trick from a Son-Life Ministries seminar, and I share it with my student and adult leadership teams every year to help engage in conversation with new visitors. Basically, get to know where they are F.R.O.M. and ask questions along these lines (almost always guaranteed to keep the conversation flowing).

- F=Family: What is your family like? Do you have any brothers? Sisters? Pets? Are you the oldest? Youngest? Middle?
- R=Recreation: What do you like to do in your spare time? Are you involved in any sports? Band? Movies? Video games?
- O=Occupation/School: What do you enjoy in school? Favorite class/least favorite class? When do you plan to graduate?
- M=Most Memorable Moment: Tell me your favorite memory from _____ (last summer, last school year, last week, etc.).

This is simple, memorable, and nonthreatening to visitors. And it opens the door to learning about that teen and helping him feel welcome.

I've shared this with teens and had them come back and tell me how effective this has been in getting to know new people who visit—especially when a youth group teen isn't sure how to connect with a newcomer. It's been a great tool for us to use for both teens and adults!

## two ideas for improving how teens welcome outsiders

Maybe this sounds a bit threatening, but try sending some of your teens to another youth group in a different community where they don't know anyone. Let them experience what it's like to be an outsider. Have them pay attention to what it feels like and what they notice about the youth group. Afterward, debrief them: Talk about what that group did that was very helpful in making them feel welcomed and what they could've improved upon. (I'm sure the youth pastor at that church would love to hear the feedback, too.)

The reverse is also helpful—find a few strangers who can come be "secret shoppers" at your youth group meeting. Again, it's best to invite teens who have no connection with anyone in your group to ensure the full we-have-a-stranger-here dynamic for your group. If you're really bold, you could even set up a hidden camera in the room and record the meeting.

Afterward, privately debrief the strangers about their impressions, how welcome the youth group made them feel, how many people talked with them, what their impressions were in the first two minutes, if they think they'd ever come back or tell a friend about the group, and so on. Then take that feedback to the group the next week and share with them what that person said. That's also a great time to show them the video that shows no one talking with the newcomer, or praise them if someone went right up to greet them as soon as they walked in the front door.

## Other Voices

### Matt Brown:

Recently several Christian leaders in a suburb of the Twin Cities met with me for consultation on holding a youth outreach in their city. In discussing the flow of an outreach-style service with them, we were at odds about several items. One leader wanted the local youth band to play before the gospel was presented. In my experience, local youth bands tend to be risky as openers because of their skill level. While Christian teens may be willing to stay and endure a poorly played song, non-Christian teens might not be so kind. I exhorted these two leaders to think very strategically from the mind of an unchurched teen. After all, when we hold a youth service geared toward them, we better have an idea about their frame of mind. While it's important to not act forced when we welcome unchurched guests to our youth service or outreach event, a little bit of putting ourselves in their shoes can go a long way.

### Tony Myles:

One idea is to swap teaching responsibilities with another youth worker in town with whom you have a healthy relationship. While everyday guests may give you everyday insights, there's nothing like a good set of "ministry" eyes and ears. Not only does this provide insights you may need, but also you can garner ideas from each other that will better your regional collective ministry.

**Ryan Nielsen:**

While I agree with this idea in theory, I don't fully agree with the execution of it. Teens are egocentric. Teens are self-absorbed. Teens are scared of being the outsider. Teens are afraid to step outside of their comfort zone. I do think this could work, but you'd need a group of self-confident teens who could handle an evaluation and critique of their behavior. I think this idea might work better if it were focused on the teen leadership team and their behavior—as the leaders of the group, the expectations for their behavior is higher. This could be very effective with student leaders, but I think could be very defeating for your average youth group attendee.

# chapter 4

# Sharing God's Word with Teens

## 10 reasons why you should do lesson preparation early

I've often said that my life is the best small group curriculum I have. Rather than coming to youth group with books and lesson materials, I simply come with stories of how God has worked in my life during the past week and Scripture that influenced my spiritual growth. For example, I may talk about a conflict I had with someone and how the Holy Spirit convicted me about it through a passage I read during my quiet time. I'll follow this up with a discussion on how we are to handle disagreements. Or maybe a Scripture passage really brought me a sense of awe and wonder last week that I'll share with the small group followed by a discussion on worship experiences in our lives.

However, while it's true that our lives provide the best material to teach our teens, it's never an excuse to come ill prepared to a place where God wants to use us to communicate his divine message.

We've all done it: driving to youth group, flipping through the Bible at every red light, hoping for some spiritual inspiration to hit us before we enter a room of teenagers (and probably church elders) who're expecting us to bring some mind-blowing truth from God's Word. It rarely works, and even when it does, you leave youth group feeling that you could've been a better steward of the time and attention that was entrusted to you.

Here are 10 reasons off the top of my head why it's best to do lesson preparation early:

1. You'll have time to meditate on the lesson so the Holy Spirit can help you tweak it.
2. There's less of a chance that you'll hit a mental block.
3. It gives you more time and ability to be creative.
4. You need the time to put the lesson into practice in your own life first before you expect others to do it. Then you'll teach from your heart instead of from your notes.
5. Teens can tell if you're prepared or not. When you are, it communicates to them that they're valuable and they'll respect you more for it.
6. Teens will take your Bible study time more seriously if they first see that you take it seriously.
7. Parents and teens will be more likely to trust your leadership in other areas of the ministry when you prove to be faithful and consistent in this significant area of ministry.
8. It's easier to teach off-script (with the Holy Spirit's promptings) when you have a clear understanding of your message as a whole.
9. There's time to promote the lesson and plug it both during private conversations and in public mass communication.
10. It communicates to everyone that God's Word is important to you and that teaching it is not a privilege you take half-heartedly.

## Other Voices

### Brian Ford:

As a speaker for camps, retreats, etc., I'm always preparing messages ahead of time even if I'm not scheduled to speak anywhere. I've learned that when God teaches me a lesson, it's also a great idea to write it down. Many sermons I've preached have come from my personal journal.

### Benjer McVeigh:

I love including teens during teaching time whenever I can. When I plan ahead, I'm able to ask a teen to prepare a three-minute testimony about how God has worked in his life relating to the topic, or I can ask a teen to prepare an illustration or activity that's right up his alley in terms of gifting.

**Tom Pounder:**

Tim, I couldn't agree with you more! When we come ill prepared it just furthers the stereotype that youth workers are just slackers who only like to play video games. In addition, when we don't prepare ahead of time, we fail to give our teens our best. I had a friend in ministry who would prepare his lesson one hour before the meeting each week! It killed me as I watched him twist and turn in his seat stressing to try to come up with something really good for the teens. Needless to say, more often than not, he came back from youth group frustrated because he didn't teach as well as he could have. We owe it to our students, the Lord, and to ourselves to properly prepare well ahead of time.

# three ideas for making God's Word "sticky"

Every youth group has the teenagers who come and lean back in their chairs with their arms crossed in front of their chest with the attitude of, "What are you going to say that I haven't already heard before?" It's frustrating for us as youth workers when God's Word seems to go in one ear and out the other, because we desperately want to see it make a difference in teens' lives.

Here are some ideas that can help make God's Word "sticky":

## Remember that relationships have a bigger impact than lectures.

I know it can be frustrating to focus on relationships when we've put our time and energy into our lessons so that we communicate God's Word as clearly and effectively as possible, but each of us has more faith in someone's opinion if it comes from a person we know and trust. We value what someone close to us has to say more than we do an acquaintance and especially more than a stranger. When a word comes from someone we're close to, her opinion matters to us.

When you tell the teens in your youth group something that will affect their spiritual lives, they'll be more likely to hear what you have to say if they trust you and love you. If you sit in your office all week and prepare a great Bible lesson but have no interaction with teens outside of church, your lesson won't have the impact you and the Lord desire.

This also means it's absolutely essential that you have a solid team of other adult leaders to help connect with teens outside of church, because as the ministry grows, you won't be able to connect with all the teens on an individual basis. You need a team of passionate and spiritually mature role models to partner with you in building spiritually influential relationships where God's Word will stick to their lives.

## God's Word must be real for you first.

Your spiritual life has to come first so that your walk with the Lord becomes contagious to the people around you. This isn't something you can just muster up and deliver from a canned Sunday school lesson—this has to be something you've internalized and is working itself out for you personally.

Not only is this essential for your own growth, but it gives God's Word credibility as you share it with teens. It's powerful when you can go to your teens and say, "I've been struggling with this issue, but then I read this in God's Word, applied it to my life, and here's how it changed me . . ." Now it's no longer just a Sunday school lesson—it's something that's real, that has practical applications, and brings credibility to the Word. This is especially true if you've already built relationships where teens care about you and your experiences.

Much of God's Word is not communicated by standing behind a music stand in the front of a youth room. You have to have a conviction that's so deep for you that it becomes contagious to the teenagers around you. It has to be more than just something you teach from a book, it has to be something that's first alive and real to you.

## You need to create experiences for learning.

We're very good at putting lesson plans together and giving talks and even leading discussions, but teenagers need to see God's Word moved outside the context of a sterile classroom.

When I worked with underprivileged inner-city teens at a camp in the early 2000s, for most of them, it was the first time they'd ever seen stars in the sky. Many of them had never seen a buffet of food before, either. They filled their plates with more food than they could possibly eat, just because they'd never seen that much food in one place. Some of them had never seen a horse—or even a squirrel—before coming to camp. They'd all heard about stars, buffets, horses, and squirrels, and they'd even seen them in movies, but it wasn't until they were at camp and actually saw them personally that their emotions were involved.

Likewise, you need to engage teenagers' emotions as they experience and learn about Scripture. Get them involved by providing experiences where not only do they learn about God's Word, but they also have to put it into practice and experience it. Take a student out to a mall and strike up a conversation with someone about God and invite the teenager into the discussion. Go on a mission trip and have a couple of teens stay back from the activity each day just so that they can pray all morning and afternoon for the ministry that's taking place with the rest of the team. During Vacation Bible School, bring the child who wants to know more about Christ to a youth group teen and ask that teen to talk with the child about it. Look for those opportunities to stretch teenagers to experience the Word and not just hear about it from a youth leader or the pastor.

In most of our own lives, we can think back on the times when life-change took place. Rarely was it because of a sermon we heard or even a small group discussion, but rather it was because of an experience we went through. And it's often the negative experiences that shape us the most. It's the feeling of being stretched beyond our capacity that God uses to mold us into his image (Romans 8:28-29). Positive experiences can have the same affect, but for some reason God likes to use trials to teach us perseverance and maturity (James 1:2-4). I'm not saying we should create negative experiences for our youth group, but when they arise (and they will), our youth groups can be places where teens can feel safe as God stretches them.

We should create an environment where God's Word is practiced, not just talked about. You and your youth ministry team can talk more about how exactly that can take place for your group. It might include feeding the homeless, going on mission trips, initiating spiritual conversations with unsaved friends, and so on. Sharing these experiences has the potential to be life changing, especially when combined with teaching and discussion.

## Other Voices

### Mike Kupferer:
Another way to make it "sticky" is to allow teens to wrestle with it. Don't give them answers right away. Don't feel like you need to prove them right or wrong. Let the questions and difficult stories marinate in their hearts and minds.

## how to push a spiritually apathetic teen to be spiritually passionate

Many people don't like the idea of pushing teens spiritually because they're afraid the teens will rebel or be turned off, but I see teens who are pushed in every area of their life except their spirituality. Their athletic coaches push them hard physically, their teachers push them academically, their jobs push them to perform, etc.

When it comes to pushing a teenager spiritually, that first hump from apathetic to interested is the hardest. That takes a lot of pushing. This is where we come alongside the teenager and say, "Hey, I know you may not care about this spiritual truth, but just try it. See if it works. See what might happen if you obey God even if you don't like what he says." If—because of your persistence—the teen gives obedience a try and he sees the Holy Spirit allow the spiritual principle he's experimenting with work out, he'll become a bit more interested. Suddenly he'll see that this God "stuff" isn't just a bunch of ideas in an old book.

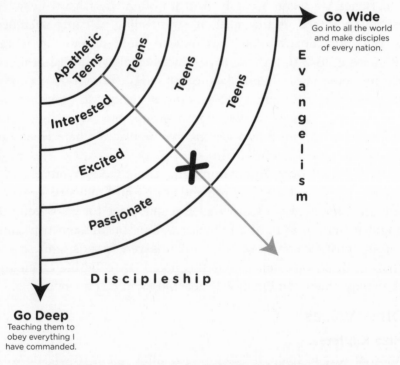

Then it'll be easier to help the teen obey in the next area of life because he'll have already seen how God's Word works when the teen's obedient. When he does it again, he'll start to become more excited about Scripture, and soon he'll be passionate about following and obeying the Lord in other areas of his life as well.

Here's the kicker: Someone who is genuinely passionate about something cannot help but share it with the people around him. I hear a lot of men talk very passionately about fishing, hunting, and car engines. It's like they wrap their entire identities around those activities. Although I care little for any of those things, I can't help but be a bit intrigued to listen to them talk about it just because they're so obviously passionate.

When someone is truly passionate about obediently following the Lord, when he wraps his entire identity around him, he'll contagiously share it with the people around him. This is one way that going deep into God's Word fits hand-in-hand with going wide.

The hump that pushed me from being spiritually apathetic to interested was sharing my faith with my peers in high school. I didn't want to share about him at all, but when I was more or less forced to do it by an adult youth leader, I was pushed to obey the Lord's command to share my faith. When I did so, I saw how following the Lord in obedience—whether I wanted to or not—really worked in my life and in the lives of others around me. I couldn't help but become a bit more interested in God and his Word. The more I shared my faith, the more spiritually excited and passionate I became.

All of us lie somewhere along the continuum of being spiritually apathetic, spiritually interested, spiritually excited, and spiritually passionate. Just do a quick gut-check and you know where you lie. Helping teens understand where they are spiritually isn't as important as helping them take the next step toward a life that is contagiously digging into Scripture and sharing Christ with the people around them. But as I've mentioned before, we should never ask teens to do something spiritually that we're not first doing ourselves. Own it, live it, and share it with teens as you journey through your spiritual lives together.

## Other Voices

### Sunnie Kim:

I think there's definitely a fear of pushing teenagers too much. I know I struggle with it each week as I lead and mentor our teenagers and our student leaders. However, because of the relationships we've built with them, they're willing to listen and at least try when my husband and I push them to seek, obey, stand out, and be challenged. Teenagers have an amazing capacity to learn and be molded with eagerness and innocence.

Last month we started a 90-day Bible reading challenge with our high school group. We called it B90X (like the P90X® extreme workout program). It's a lot of reading (12-16 chapters a day), but I've been amazed at how they've been doing it so diligently, asking questions, encouraging each other, even reading ahead! Even the teenagers I thought weren't going to do it are asking me if I'm on schedule (right now I'm behind!).

We also push the teens to be obedient not just at church but also in all aspects of their lives. We've challenged them to be holy—even on Facebook. I immediately saw a lot less swearing, complaining, and unkindness on my Facebook newsfeed.

It's a beautiful thing to see teens growing in their knowledge of Christ and in their passion for him. It definitely takes a while, but I think that modeling, relationship-building, passion, and pushing—not to mention a ton of praying—really do help lead teens from apathetic to passionate.

### Jeremy Zach:

I'm with you. When we spiritually lead adolescents, they need a sense of structure and support. I've found that if you raise the bar, they'll most likely meet you there.

Bottom line: Discipleship happens from the inside out.

The fundamental question every youth pastor wrestles with is: How can our youth ministries cultivate and facilitate passion within our teens?

I think there's a two-part answer:

1. Raise the bar.
2. Put teens in an environment that cultivates wonder.

Wonder is connected with God and produces in the soul a sense of awe and adoration. Students should not only want to worship God, but also desire to obey God. When the Holy Spirit is present inside our teen's hearts, souls, and minds, that's passion!

### Tim's response to Jeremy:

Sounds great, but could you give me some ideas of what you mean by putting adolescents in an environment of wonder? It sounds like something I'd love to do, but in my own life those environments are usually when I step out in faith, take risks, and leave my comfort zone and see God come through when I'm forced to depend on him. Are you thinking we should do more to somehow place teens in those kinds of situations?

**Jeremy's response to Tim:**

Exactly. You mix up your youth ministry environments. Once teens get in a routine, it's time to change it up. This is why variety is huge. I am suggesting we throw our teens into at least one or two new faith environments every quarter. Here are some practical examples:

1. During youth group, leave the church building and go evangelize in a public place.
2. Go visit another Jesus-believing church that's very different from your church. Look for different cultural experiences.
3. Go to different camps, retreats, and events. I know some youth ministries have sacred cows, but change it up.
4. Challenge the teens to be silent for 30 minutes during youth group as they try to listen to God.
5. Invite your teens to run the entire youth group night. Don't do this a lot, but do it enough so they can get comfortable ministering to others.

Honestly, in my experience the two biggest ways to create wonder is by allowing the teens to be still before God and by challenging them to minister to others whom they wouldn't normally minister to.

# three things teens should know before they graduate

As youth workers, most of us realize that our time with teens is limited. If we're not careful, we could spend our brief years of Bible studies and youth group meetings randomly jumping from topic to topic, verse to verse, and when high school graduation comes around they'll have learned a lot of jumbled facts.

Your time with teens is short and very valuable, so it's important to think through some big-picture questions such as, By the time my teens graduate from high school, what should they know? Where should they be spiritually? What should their lives look like? Use these questions to help you develop a plan for how to help move them spiritually from point A in 7th grade to point B in 12th grade.

Obviously, this is ultimately a work of the Holy Spirit. We're all depraved beings and our natural desire is to pursue things that oppose God, so while I would love to see three things take place in every graduating senior in my ministry, I first have to be honest enough to say that these three things aren't always present in my own life. My sin constantly derails me from being a perfect example for teens.

However, without assuming too much responsibility for how each teen chooses to respond to the Holy Spirit's promptings, there are a few things our ministry does to help push teenagers toward each of the three things. (These are only examples of my ministry based on my church's values. You should discuss the above questions with your pastor and adult leaders to determine your own direction for the ministry. Of course, like any list of goals, they need to be specific, measurable, and attainable.)

## 1. What we want teens to know: An overview understanding of the entire Bible.

I'm not saying they need to know everything in Scripture, but they should at least be able to track through Genesis to Revelation with a general understanding of how it all ties together. Biblical literacy is key because you can't fall in love with someone if you don't know much about him. But the more you know, the more there is to fall in love with, and the more you fall in love, the more you want to know about that person. Knowing God's Word is foundational to knowing and loving God.

**What we do to push them toward this: 7th and 8th graders go through the entire Bible before high school.**

Our junior high small groups use a course called The Journey that takes 7th and 8th graders through the entire Old Testament one year and the New Testament the next. By the time they enter high school, they have a basic understanding of the entire Word of God. Small group leaders do their best to help the junior high students not just fill their head with facts. Daily journaling, reflection, memorization, acts of service, and more help them practically apply it all to their daily life and practice.

## 2. What we want teens to know: How to study Scripture for themselves.

I don't want our youth group teens to graduate and always be dependent on someone else to chew on God's Word, digest it, and spit it out in bite-size pieces for them each week at church. I want them to learn how to feed on the Word of God for their own and not just swallow the assumptions that I—or any other pastor or teacher—throw at them. They should be equipped to dig into God's Word on their own, study it for themselves, and feed on its life-sustaining power—we don't want them to be content with spiritual milk.

**What we do to push them toward this: Teach Bible study methods to high schoolers.**

This is a hard balance for me. Last year I did an eight-week series on hermeneutics and basically taught a crash course of my Intro to Bible Study Methods class from Dallas Theological Seminary. I whipped out all my old notes, gave them some of the same homework assignments I had in seminary, and provided books for further study. A few teenagers stepped up to the challenge and really took the observation, interpretation, and application process very seriously. For other teens, however, it was over their head. I plan to revisit this series again, but I'll simplify it and move it to the context of a small group instead of large-group teaching so there can be better interaction.

## 3. What we want teens to know: Worship and evangelism should be a natural part of their daily lives.

1 Corinthians 8:1 says, "Knowledge puffs up while love builds up." And 1 Corinthians 4:20 says, "For the kingdom of God is not a matter of talk but of power." Learning God's Word and being able to study it on your own is great, but if that knowledge is just a lot of talk and never turns to love for God and for people (i.e., the Great Commandment), then it's a waste. The outpouring of their knowledge of God should turn into a passionate love that's exemplified in their worship and their burden for lost people.

**What we do to push them toward this: Youth leaders must model personal worship and evangelism.**

I do my best never to ask my teens to do something that I haven't first tried in my own life. That means if I'm going to ask them to share about a time in the previous week when they brought God up in a conversation with an unsaved friend, I'd better have a story to share as well. If I'm challenging them to dig into God's Word, I need to be doing it first and sharing that experience with the teens. They need to see how studying God's Word plays out in my own life, how it affects my own decisions and values, and how it's reflective in my personal worship and outreach. Otherwise I'm just another Christian hypocrite.

What it all really comes down to is our youth group's vision to go deep into God's Word and wide with his message to the people around us. That's what drives everything we do, including the three things I want my teens to know before they graduate.

## Other Voices

### Mike Andrews:

I just finished a series dealing with five elements that have seemed to consistently be a part of my teaching over the years. Before they graduate, I want my teens' lives to be characterized by:

1. A permanent attitude of worship.
2. A global view of God's church.
3. A passion for revealing God to people who don't notice him.
4. A commitment to local service as the church.
5. A hunger for depth in their relationship to God.

### Brett Hetherington:

I'd say this list is pretty solid. I might add to it that I hope teens learn not to rely on their American perceptions of the church.

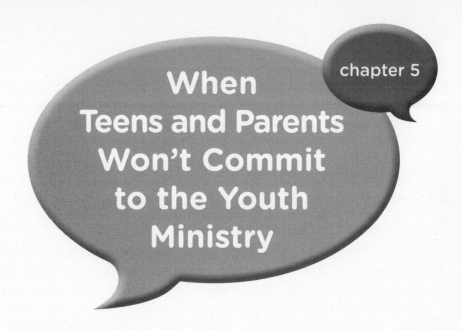

# When Teens and Parents Won't Commit to the Youth Ministry

chapter 5

## what teens and parents will and won't commit to

### People don't commit to programs—they commit to relationships.

Often, one of the first questions a teenager asks before signing up for a youth trip is, "Who else is going?" Most people don't care about the program, the trip, or the event as much as they care about the people they'll be with. How is your ministry leveraging relationships with teens—both peer relationships and adult relationships? Does the program serve the spiritually encouraging relationships, or do the people serve the program?

### People don't commit to programs—they commit to vision.

People rally behind a vision—rarely behind a program. Passionately communicate the vision for your ministry and get people on board with that. When the vision is contagious and people understand how they fit into the big overall picture, then they'll become excited about the program that may guide them there. People want to be part of a movement—something that's significant and is bigger than they are. Where is your youth ministry going? How compelling is the direction? Are you passionate about it? Or is it just a statement typed on a piece of paper?

Programs are here to serve the relationships, the vision of your ministry, and ultimately to bring glory to God as a body of Christ—not the other way around. If you're spending a lot of energy trying to get people to commit to your programs, you have it all backward.

It should never be about the program in the first place.

## Other Voices

**Tony Myles:**

I used to believe that it was the youth worker's role to be a visionary leader. These days I'm more convinced that we need to each be a "leader of visions." What I mean is that it's much better to see the vision God is establishing in individual people and find ways to glue them together as a mosaic instead of demanding that everyone follow you. Ask teens and adult leaders questions like, "What's one thing you would remove and one thing you would add to what we do?" Their answers may sting a bit, but if you're smart you'll pick up on something each person says that you can respond to by saying, "I like that idea. How can I help you take hold of that?"

**Ryan Nielsen:**

In the 1980s, programs brought teens in and programs kept them. If you wanted a large youth group, you put on amazing programs. In the 1990s, programs brought teens in, but relationships kept them there. Today, relationships bring teens in and relationships keep them (both peer relationships and adult relationships). The teens are not drawn as much by the amazing programs as they are by people who care about them personally. That's what'll draw them in, and that's what'll keep them. Thus, relationships need to be a high priority.

**Paul Turner:**

Programs are excuses for relationships. I've been feeling lately that maintaining a youth group is too small of a vision—yet, that's what many churches want. We should all be open to the wild call of God that will lead to a mission beyond our imagination.

# handling teenagers who don't want to participate in youth group activities

We all have them in our church: teenagers who don't want to participate in the youth group and parents who are noncommittal about serving, helping, or even encouraging their teens to attend.

How do I handle teenagers who don't want to participate in youth activities? The short answer: Generally speaking, I don't do much. Instead, I focus my energy on those who are excited about where the group is going. However, I always reach out to those who don't participate in order to catch up with them and make sure they know they're always welcome. It's important to build a relationship with them, so I'll ask one of the adult volunteers to be intentional about contacting them through comments on their Facebook pictures, text messages saying they're praying for them today, and so on. But I don't have a program in place to do anything more than that.

There's often a variety of reasons why teens might not want to be involved in youth group: relational conflict, they don't see the value in it, other things are demanding their time, and so on. It's important to talk through some of those reasons with those teens—not so you can convince them that their reasons are wrong, but so they feel that their voice is heard and valued. Remember, the point isn't to get them to attend your group as much as it is to encourage them spiritually. If they don't get that encouragement at youth group, maybe it can happen outside of the normal meeting times.

Two things not to do:

1. Don't guilt them into coming. Don't say something to the effect of, "Jamie thinks you're stuck-up because you won't come to youth group." Guilt will never work to your advantage—it's manipulation. Instead try, "We miss seeing you on Wednesday nights—I really enjoyed that one time you came."
2. Don't pressure them. Just listen, hear them out, and don't take it personally if they think you and your ministry are lame. If they have some valid suggestions about ways you could change the ministry, do it. Better yet, use the teenager to implement the change. But don't beg them to come every week. Give them open-ended invitations when appropriate, and otherwise listen to them, pray for them, and give them some spiritual attention outside of youth group.

## Other Voices

### Erica Hoagland:

I'm wondering to what extent parents who are members of a church body should be held accountable for their students not attending

Sunday school or youth group activities. This is a current debate in our youth ministry. Most of the teen children of members of our church don't engage in our programs and when we ask their parents why, the common answer is, "I'm not going to force them to come." Is this something that we as youth leaders should accept? If teens didn't want to attend school, would the same logic apply? I'm honestly just looking for feedback on this debate, as I'm not sure where I should stand on this issue.

**Tim's response to Erica:**

That's a good issue to bring up, Erica. Basically there are three things I think you need to address:

1. The spiritual apathy of the parents. Typically the parents who give the response you receive are spiritually apathetic themselves. Addressing that should become your first priority because if parents aren't being spiritual role models at home, you're fighting an uphill battle. Spiritually apathetic parents almost always mean apathetic teens, which means teens who'll drop out of church altogether after high school.

2. The perceived value of what you're doing. Do you have a vision for where you're going with the youth ministry? Are you taking the ministry in a direction that excites people? Do you have a vision they can take ownership of? People don't commit to programs—they commit to movements. You may need to really seek the Lord for that vision and communicate it often, clearly, and concisely.

3. Create a community teens want to be a part of. If teenagers don't want to be part of your youth ministry, don't take it personally, but do take it seriously if it's the majority of teens in your church. What misconceptions do they have? What about the ministry is unattractive to teens? I do know one thing: Every teen wants to feel unconditionally loved, valued, and safe. If you can create that kind of community with your teens, every teenager in your town will want to be a part of it.

It starts with you. Model it yourself: Grow in ways you want the teens to grow, risk the things you want them to risk, ask the questions of your own life that you ask them to ask about theirs. Model the vulnerability you want them to share with you (within reason, of course).

And most importantly, seek the Lord's direction for the ministry, become passionate about it so it's contagious to others, follow his plan for how to get there, put the plan in place, and communicate it with everyone you know.

**Joel Diaz:**

I needed to hear this. I moved to a new church in January and there are some teens who have not been regular attendees. They show up on the church campus, but don't want to participate in the larger group. It was frustrating, and I started to take it personally. What I did is start going to their schools for lunch. I would meet up with the teens who did want to see me, and the teens who typically didn't participate in youth group would sometimes join us. I now have some of those teens showing up for our youth group night.

## handling frustrations about low attendance

Years ago when I was growing up in a Sunday school where attendance was sketchy at best, it was not uncommon for me to hear the teacher ask, "Where is everybody?" with a poorly hidden tone of disappointment. My teacher would then proceed to ask more questions about why certain people were absent than he would about those who were present. Sometimes I felt that if I wanted the teacher to pay attention to me, it was better to skip Sunday school.

I learned a valuable lesson from those experiences: Rather than focus on those who are absent, always be excited about the teens who are present.

Don't enter a room and ask, "Where is everyone?" The teens present will be thinking, "What about me? I'm here!" Instead, enter a room and focus on every student who is there and is interested in the Word you have to bring. Even if you put 30 hours into your Bible study lesson for the week, don't skip it or abbreviate it because only a handful of teens showed up. Feed those who came and make them feel as welcome as you possibly can.

When you enter the youth room, focus on the teens who are present. After word spreads around about how accepted and welcomed the minority feels, everyone else will be back. (Of course, it's always a good idea to follow up with the absent teens during the week, too.)

### Other Voices

**David Schmoyer:**

I never really thought about this as an adult, but looking back at the youth group/Sunday school experiences in my past, I did experience many of the feelings you described. I was there every Sunday because I had to be, but it made a huge difference when the leader showed that he was glad I was there and that he was excited to be there, too.

**Mike Kupferer:**

What I've found funny over the past year or so is that I have to answer the teens' questions about where everyone is. I try not to focus on those who aren't there, but there have been times when those who are in attendance will ask, "Where is everyone?" After I laugh a little to myself, I realize that this statement reinforces the fact that relationships are vitally important to teenagers. I try to answer the question by saying something like, "You're all here, so let's get started." Next time you want to ask, "Where is everyone?" stop and make a note of who you don't see, and then contact them within a day to let them know they were missed.

**Justin Ross:**

Just last month, youth group was kicking off in 10 minutes and no one had shown up yet. A teen who'd been coming for just a few weeks wandered in, and as I greeted him, the first thing he said (with a little bit of panic in his voice) was, "Where is everyone else?" I replied, "I don't know where they are, but I've been waiting on you. I saw this video on YouTube you have to see."

We went in my office, and I pulled up a funny video I thought he'd like. As we were watching it, other teens began to show up.

I have no doubt that if I had said, "I don't know where everyone is; I guess no one is coming tonight," he would have been on his phone telling his mom to turn around and come get him. Instead, now he tells me about a new YouTube video every week.

## should you use a reward system for youth group attendance?

When youth group attendance seems to be lacking, the temptation is to try to give it a little shot in the arm by providing incentives for teens to come and bring friends. When I was in high school I remember one of the leaders saying he would shave his mustache off if we could double the size of our class by the end of the summer. The only problem was that no one really cared if he shaved his mustache off.

If he had offered us an Xbox or an HDTV instead, would we have actually followed through on inviting friends and asking them to come for the summer? Maybe. But would it have kept us there? Would this even be something appropriate to do?

If you've thought about using a reward system for youth group attendance, let me help you to avoid a big mistake: Do not offer bribes for teens coming to youth group. A reward system will ultimately fail because there's no way you can compete with their alternatives (video games, movies, TV shows, going to the mall, concerts, etc.). In fact, a reward system will only encourage teens to come for selfish reasons, which is not at all what the body of Christ is supposed to be all about. Plus, it's only a matter of time until your reward is no longer a big deal to anyone and you'll have to come up with something bigger and better in order to keep the teens' attention. You can't keep that up for long.

Let me suggest two better tactics:

1. Build personal relationships with the teens you're in touch with.
2. Facilitate an environment where those teens can build relationships with each other.

As I've said before, people don't often go to church because they want to hear the music, listen to a sermon, or because of cool church events. People primarily go to church because of the relationships they have there with other people.

Teenagers are the same way. They want to be where their friends are, whether that's at school, the mall, online, or at church. So use that to your advantage by getting to know the teens personally and by facilitating relationships between them. If your youth group teens enjoy each other and you, they'll come.

Some practical ways to do this:

1. Rather than expecting teens to come to you, go to them instead. Hang out on their campus, their homes, and have them over to your house. Be sure you don't talk about youth group unless they ask. You're not there to market your programs—you're there to love your teenagers.
2. If you only have two teenagers who do come to youth group, take them out for ice cream and talk. Let them get to know each other. If you have only one teen, take him out and get to know him personally. (If the teen is a girl and you're a guy, take a female adult with you so you're not alone with the teen. Being alone with any female who isn't your wife is

a recipe for disaster, even if you stay in a public place. And if you're a female youth worker, the reverse is true.)

3. Every relationship revolves around trust. The thing about trust is that it's not handed over to you just because you're a youth pastor. Trust is something you earn over time. So be patient and earn your group's respect.

## Other Voices

### Jeff Smith:

I totally agree . . . and disagree. No, you can't compete with what the teens can get on their own or through their parents. No, you shouldn't bribe them to come to church.

On the other hand, rewards for a major push wouldn't be so bad. Maybe a very cool prize for bringing the most new teens in a three-month period, or really any kind of prize. For some it's just the idea of winning rather than the prize. I did a PowerPoint game and the prize was a rubber chicken key chain I got free at a Youth Specialties National Youth Workers Convention. You would have thought I'd given them some major money.

Jesus healed people and then spoke truth to them. He rewarded them for coming, then preached the Word to them. I think you find a balance. Yes, you want to build relationships, and you want them to come because they want to—and feel they need to—come. But, some healthy bribes along the way won't hurt. Treat the baby believers like baby believers sometimes. We bribed our children to use the potty—until they grew up and started using it because it was the right thing to do.

There is no cut-and-dried answer to this one. I say do it if it fits the situation and teens, but don't overdo it. Help them grow, but recognize they're still children and many are probably babies in the faith. That's okay. Don't expect them to grow up overnight.

### Grahame Knox's response to Jeff:

Jeff, I'm sorry to disagree with you. Is there such a thing as a "healthy" bribe? I'm not sure. Should we give a prize to someone who brings the most teens? Or should we teach our young people more about the privilege of sharing God's love and the good news of Jesus with their school friends? Also, I'm really not sure about your analysis that when Jesus healed people he was rewarding them for coming and listening to his words. I've always thought he healed them because he loved them whether they listened to what he said or not.

I guess my concern is about what I'll call "consumer-oriented" youth ministry. Should we be encouraging teens to think, "What can I get if . . . ?" or "What can I win if . . . ?" Isn't the Christian life more about serving? Isn't it more about giving than receiving?

**Jon Eagleson:**

The way I see it, having "bring people" as your primary goal makes numbers your primary objective. If you have "get to know people and have fun" as one of your primary goals, then your youth will develop "bring people" as one of their goals, because they're enjoying the program. And if you've motivated the youth to do it, it'll get done a lot better than if you're trying to push your own motivation on them.

**Justin Ross:**

"The only problem was, no one really cared if he shaved his mustache off." This made me laugh because I remember being at a youth group meeting at the end of my senior year of high school and the youth pastor saying if enough people signed up for camp, he would let his wife build an ice cream sundae on his head. I remember how immediately my whole group of friends began talking about how that was the most ridiculous thing we'd ever heard. It was certainly not something any of us cared to see.

## parents who ground their teens from youth group

It's always an interesting dynamic when parents ground their teenagers from youth group. One would assume that if the teen is having issues, then church is exactly where he needs to be. But nonetheless, it's quite common for parents to restrict youth group activities as a form of punishment.

GiGi Logan, the children's and youth ministry director at All Saint's Episcopal Church in North Carolina, wrote me in an email, ". . . parents don't realize that they're teaching their teens that church is like a cell phone or a TV and that's so not cool!"

A few observations:

1. While I'm excited that a teenager enjoys youth group enough for the parents to see it as a significant loss for their child, it's still exactly that—a significant loss. Teens aren't grounded from going to school, because attending school is both a privilege and a responsibility. Church is no different.

2. I'm against using church as punishment. This isn't because I'm a youth pastor. I'm against it because the church is instituted by God and every student here is an important part of the body.

3. Always support the parents in front of their teens. If you want to talk through the issues surrounding the teens' grounding from church, do it privately with the parents. Approach the conversation with humility and ask questions about the situation rather than opening with statements about how you disagree with their parenting methods. Find ways to partner with the parents through the situation.

## Other Voices

### Jason Curlee:

In 14 years of working with teens this has always been the hardest situation I experience. I've always equated it with grounding a diabetic teen from her insulin.

Parents' rationale is that teens enjoy youth group, so it makes sense to ground them from it. I personally think that's the lamest excuse. If you feel comfortable enough, I would suggest that you start a dialogue with the parent to get a better understanding of the situation. You might be able to help the parents come up with a more creative way to discipline.

Part of our role is also pastoring the parents God has given us.

### Calvin Park:

When a teen in my youth ministry is grounded from normal youth ministry gatherings, I typically try to speak with the parents. I think most of the time this grounding takes place because parents don't completely understand the role youth ministry is meant to take in the lives of their teens. Often they view youth group as another extracurricular activity: It's not a spiritual thing, it's a fun thing.

### Lori Still:

Even if youth group is the only valuable thing the teen has, grounding should still not be the discipline of choice. Parents need to get creative. What's the teen grounded for? If she's grounded because of her grades, then make her go to the school tutor in the morning before class or after school until her grades improve. Is she fighting with siblings? If so, make her do something extraordinarily nice for the siblings for a period of time—make them breakfast, clean their rooms, and so on. The discipline could teach something, not just be a loss of something valuable.

**Dave Burkholder:**

As I was reading these comments I was thinking about marketing. How are we marketing our youth ministry? Are we highlighting the fun aspects or the spiritual aspects? In our youth group, it's not uncommon for our teens to be grounded for a month, yet be allowed to come to youth group. I believe the reason for this is the perception our youth workers have instilled in the parents' minds that church is the only thing that's going to help their teen change. Many of our parents are at their wits' end with their teens and are looking anywhere for a solution to behavior problems. We, as a church, can offer a solution.

Chapter 6

# Communication

## five tips to remember when sharing youth group announcements

### 1.Be aware that communication is a fine art that always seems to be morphing.

A few years in a row I presented a seminar called Communicating with Teens and Parents Throughout the Week at the Simply Youth Ministry Conference, and every year I had to significantly update the content. Each time I reviewed my notes from the previous year, it was shocking how outdated my information had become. Communication methods change quickly as technology changes, new tools are introduced, and existing tools evolve.

It's easy to look at communication over the span of decades and see how the printed word transitioned to the telegraph, which transitioned to the telephone, which made way for the Internet and social media, but we often fail to see the subtle shifts that slowly outdate our communication methods.

Because communication methods are always changing, the next tip is crucial:

### 2. You must always evaluate your communication methods.

I'll confess I've only been evaluating our ministry's communication methods for a couple of years now. I used to just take other people's successful ideas and copy them in my own ministry expecting the same outstanding results. But culture varies from one part of the country to another—even from church to church in the same community—so you can't expect to always be able to use the same communication methods successfully.

When I worked at a church in Texas, email worked perfectly for us because almost everyone had Smartphones. If I sent a message out, I had responses back from almost all my leaders within an hour. But when I moved to Minnesota, not only did most people not have Smartphones, they also only checked email about once a week. Some people didn't use email at all.

I started tracking the results of what worked and didn't work in my youth group. In the next section I'll share some of my approaches along with how I evaluated the results, so that you can determine what might work best for your ministry context.

### 3. On some level, your audience has a responsibility to be proactive.

You can be the best communicator in the world, but at some point your audience has the responsibility to receive your message. You can't embed your youth group announcements directly into someone's brain, and you can't make the updated event information post itself on everyone's refrigerator.

While I know many of our churches expect us to spoon-feed our teens the information they want the way they want it, that's an unrealistic expectation—especially as your group grows. Relieve yourself of that expectation right now.

You can and should do everything you can to make the information readily available in a format that's easy for them to consume, but teenagers still need to take the initiative to get the information and put it on their own calendars.

I serve a group of about 200 teenagers, and every once in a while I get a parent who says, "We'd prefer it if you could just call us each week and update Johnny about what's going on with the youth group." My response is always no. All the information is readily available in multiple formats. Pick which one works best for you and go with that.

Which leads to the fourth tip:

## 4. Communication methods may take some training.

This is especially true if you've done some evaluating and determined that you need to eliminate one of your communication methods and replace it with something else.

For example, maybe the amount of time you were putting into postcard mailings just wasn't worth the time and expense anymore, but you have three vocal families in your ministry who demand you continue the mailings.

One approach is that you continue the postcards for a period of time while transitioning to bulletin inserts. Then cut off the postcards because they're just not working like they used to. Then you have to train people to look to the bulletins instead.

Sometimes training people where to find the right information takes time, but it's a very necessary part of communicating well.

Communicating well means three things:

- You must continually reinforce where people can find information.
- Be consistent with where you put information. You can't publish it on Facebook one week, in the bulletin the next, and on your blog another week.
- Publish information on a regular schedule so people learn when to expect it. I try to get all of our youth group's information published on Tuesday so they know when to check the website, email, and Facebook for news and announcements. It becomes a part of their weekly routine.

## 5. Communication is credibility.

There are two things that are vitally important to any youth ministry: relationships and communication. This is perhaps the most important part of why good communication is so essential to youth ministries. Way too many ministries miss this.

A youth worker can be a great person, beloved by all the teens, and an effective teacher of God's Word, but if he communicates poorly with the parents and other church staff members throughout the week, his credibility will be weak because no one will be quite sure what's going on. When people feel disconnected, they tend to lose trust in their leader.

Conversely, a youth leader may not be a hero to the teens and may be just an average teacher, but if she communicates effectively and consistently with parents and church staff throughout the week, there's a greater level of perceived credibility because people will feel like they know what's going on.

Whether you like it or not, how well you communicate really does impact the perceived level of credibility people have of you and your ministry.

## Other Voices

### Tony Myles:

We're all stronger in one area of communication, which means we all have room to grow in another. Perhaps you can easily rally people on the spot to a vision or event, or maybe you're more able to maximize print and electronic forms of communication. Whatever your strength, find someone who excels in your weak area and ask them to proof your communication before you send it out. What you think is comprehensive information may still be short of details that others might care about.

Remember that good communication in ministry isn't just about passing along information—it's about communicating vision. Think about it—why should a teen give her life to something she doesn't fully understand?

### Lars Rood:

I was listening to some announcements at a new church I was visiting. The person giving the announcements made me not want to be involved with what they were talking about because it sounded like the most boring thing ever. I don't think we always need to have 200 percent energy when we're sharing announcements—that can seem fake, too. But at least talk to teens in a way that shows that you get the world they live in and that the announcements you're making have some sort of relevance to their world.

## evaluating your ministry's communication methods

I usually don't make announcements at youth group. There's nothing wrong with the groups that do, I just choose not to because, for my group, that "info download" time can take place just as easily (and more effectively) through a variety of other means. I don't like to take time away from our lesson, worship, or fun time together for it.

Here's a quick summary of how I communicate with my parents and teens in my youth group during the week, including my method of evaluating each one's effectiveness. Keep in mind that the findings are from my own youth group only. Every youth group and every area of the country will have different results. It's important that you test your methods with your group and not just adopt mine, because what works for my teens may not work with yours.

Some of the results may be surprising to you.

From worst to best:

## 6. Mass Facebook messages

Primary Audience: High school students

It surprised me to find that mass Facebook messages are absolutely the worst form of communication I have with my teens. I have a typical Facebook page set up, and every week I send out an update with information that pertains mostly to high school students. I try to keep the messages brief and to the point so that the teens can find the information they need. I wanted to track how many teens were actually opening the messages, so I started sending just the main headings of the announcements and included a link to more details on our website. I found that the click-through rate was about two percent.

I used a self-hosted URL shortener called Get Shorty to track the number of times my links were clicked, but you could just as easily use something like bit.ly, too, which is what I use for Twitter, actually.

If only two percent of the teens actually click the link in Facebook to get the info they want, that method is pretty much worthless for us.

## 5. Mass email

Primary Audience: Parents

Most teens here don't use email, so this is for the few teens who do use it and for all the parents. When I write up our weekly youth group news and announcements, I publish it to the front page of our youth group website and shortly thereafter a service called Feedblitz automatically sends it as an email to everyone on the mailing list.

Feedblitz has some tracking tools that show that the open rate of my emails is about 20 percent. I know that sounds good compared to the Facebook messages, but that still means that 80 percent of the parents are not even opening my weekly email messages. And of the 20 percent who actually open the email (either accidentally or on purpose), an even smaller number of them click through to get more information.

So, email doesn't seem to be a great solution for us, either.

## 4. Bulletin insert/Youth kiosk
Primary Audience: Church visitors

Since every newcomer to our church on Sunday mornings takes a bulletin, we include a youth group news insert that gives an overview that pertains mostly to someone who is a first-time visitor and wants to know more about the youth ministry.

We also have a youth kiosk right outside the main doors of our Worship Center (sanctuary) with more handouts. This serves as the hub of our information center at church. This is where we keep handouts, flyers, contact forms, sign-up sheets, and so on. It also has the current week's youth group news video playing in a loop (we'll talk about that in a minute).

Unfortunately, there's no real way to track the effectiveness of bulletin inserts or our youth kiosk—but using them is very low maintenance, so we continue to use them. The insert is mostly a tweaked copy-and-paste of the email update I post to our website early in the week, so it's not a lot of extra work.

## 3. Website
Primary Audience: Parents and junior high students

I'm not really sure why the high school teens don't utilize our website very often, but regardless, they don't.

Our site's traffic statistics show that the site is getting over 100 visitors and about 1,500 page loads every day. That means that the average visitor clicks through approximately 15 pages on the site before leaving. That's a very high click-through rate for any website. (My blog, by contrast, gets about two clicks from each visitor.) People are definitely visiting our site and looking for information there. In fact, whenever there's a typo or an incorrect calendar date, we hear about it pretty quickly.

## 2. Video announcements
Primary Audience: Parents, high school students, and junior high students

Last year I started experimenting with communicating youth group news and announcements through video and made a few observations:

- If I stood in front of the teens and made an announcement, most of them tuned me out. However, if I said the exact same thing on a screen, they all listened intently.
- Plugging videos into iTunes makes it simple for teens to sync them to their MP3 players to watch whenever they want.
- Adding more content to the videos than just news makes it a highlight of youth group for some teens.
- There's a reason why YouTube and online video is so huge with teens—let's utilize it!

Yes, creating videos takes more time than writing a simple email, but if it actually communicates, then it's worth the time.

The statistics for each video's views and downloads at YouTube, Blip.tv, and Facebook equals a lot more than the number of teenagers we have in our youth ministry, which probably means that teens are watching the episodes several times each week and that their friends are watching them, too. In fact, I often hear from people in our community who don't even attend our church but watch our youth group videos online. Our message definitely spreads farther via video than any other communication method we have. (Hint: Get some of your youth group teens in the video and (with their parents' permission) tag them in it on Facebook. The video is then more likely to show up in a lot of their friends' news feed, making it easy to use video to communicate with many more teenagers than just your youth group.)

For teenagers who don't have high-speed Internet at home, I also show the video each week at youth group if there's time for it.

## 1. Mass text messages
Primary Audience: High school students

Text messaging is by far our number one most effective means of communication. We use it for many things:

- Announcements and last-minute reminders
- Event cancellations (works great when the weather forces you to change plans on the spot)
- Birthday wishes
- Bible verses and short devotionals
- Contests, quizzes, and polls
- Prayer chain prayer requests and praise reports
- Introduction to the weekend's upcoming lesson
- To request feedback about an idea or question

I send mass text messages out at pretty random times, too. When teens are off from school, I'll sometimes send a message, "The first three people to reply to this message get a free lunch with me and Dana today. We'll pick you up at 12:30 p.m." Within minutes my reply box lights up (which is good for my self-esteem, too).

The only limitations with text messaging are that I must be very concise, and that not every teen or parent in our group has text messaging available. But for the ones who do have it, it's hands-down the best communication method we have—quick communication with instant responses.

## Other Voices

**Josh Frank:**

I have our non-texting teens saved as a group in my cell phone, so it's easy for me to call them right before or after sending a text out to the teens who do text. It's much easier for me to remember to call the people I need to call if they're saved as a group in my phone.

**Matt Parker:**

Don't forget the always-popular word of mouth. We've found that if we can get the teens talking to their friends (as you pointed out with your videos), news will spread like wildfire.

# guidelines for youth pastors who text teens

As a general rule of thumb, I don't let my ministry be crippled by the fear of what could happen. I take prudent precautions, of course, but there's a limit where you'll soon have no contact with teens at all, and they might start to feel like you're afraid of them.

I text my teenagers. I usually only text girls to ask a quick question, but I don't have ongoing discussions with them—even if they initiate the text conversation. I'll gladly reply and answer questions, but I don't prolong the small talk (and infrequent), "So how was your day?" texts from girls. I'd rather see that conversation take place with a female youth leader.

As far as guys are concerned, I've not had to place guidelines on those conversations yet. I'm sure there are some teenage guys out there who would require a youth leader to lay down some restrictions, though.

My advice: Do what you feel is right for your ministry rather than crippling your ministry with the fear of what could happen. But at the same time, be prudent and wise.

If your ministry requires some accountability in your texting with teens, consider using a group text messaging and archiving service. (I use TxtSignal.com.) These companies will enable you to keep a record of your conversations. If there's ever a question about your texting with a teen, you can go back and check the original transcripts.

## Other Voices

### Mike Nagel:

The one thing I do with texting or emailing girls (a piece of advice given to me by another youth pastor) is to say "we" instead of "I." It's always "We missed you last week" versus "I missed you last week." It helps keep perspective and distance without just putting a complete stop to communication. And it works out well because my wife is also a youth leader, so she's included in the conversation, too.

### David Plumley:

We had to draft an entire policy on this. We reach out to hundreds of teenagers in our community—most of whom receive text messages from us. However, there are a couple parents who don't think we should be texting at all (they see us as within a public school teacher type of relationship where teachers shouldn't be texting teens). To avoid any issues, we had to implement a new policy with one key item: parental permission. Parents sign a form that says they give permission for us to text their child. It may be a lot of work to get all the forms, but it's working in our situation and provides accountability.

### Ruth Elkin:

There are so many fears regarding interacting with youth through technological forms of communication like text, email, and social networks—but not so much around the traditional forms of communication like letters and phone calls. In some ways this is a justified fear when we see how people exploit others through these mediums, but these communication tools can be used safely and successfully. This all said, it's important to keep a record of anything exchanged via technological means due to misunderstandings and misinterpretations that so easily happen. It's important to meet teens where they are and to build relationships with them, but safeguarding ourselves and them is crucial to building good relationships not only with our young people, but also with their families. As a part of this parents need to be aware that you are communicating with their teenager through text, email, social networks, and so on.

chapter 7

# Managing Money

## writing a youth ministry budget

Although many youth ministries don't really have a budget that requires more than five minutes of, "Hmm . . . should we spend it all on a large pizza or save it for Advil after the lock-in?" it seems to be a common question: How do I put together a youth ministry budget?

Here are some tips for developing your budget:

### Tip #1: Carefully think through curriculum.

You should do this anyway, not just from a financial standpoint, but also for the sake of your teenagers' spiritual development. Are you hopping from one topic to whatever else your teens want to learn about? If so, you must develop a plan and a vision for where you want to take your teens through Scripture and how you're going to get there. Otherwise, you'll waste a lot of money on curriculum that won't take your students in any particular direction.

Also, think about whether or not you need to purchase curriculum, or if you can write it in-house. Curriculum is expensive, and honestly, some of it isn't worth your money. Taking an extra 30 minutes a week to put your own Bible study together is not only free, but may offer about 10 times the impact of a generic, one-size-fits-all discussion sheet.

## Tip #2: Invest in leaders.

The best use of any size youth ministry budget is to invest it in your adult leaders. In fact, at my previous church, I saved my entire annual budget each year so I could spend 100 percent of it on training and appreciation gifts. A team of adult leaders who are passionate for teens, well-trained, mature, and equipped to be effective tools of the Holy Spirit is by far the greatest blessing your budget can provide for teens. That goes so much farther than a few pizzas and some cool youth events.

If you're the only youth worker in your church, don't be bashful in using the entire budget on yourself. Use it to buy ministry books, attend youth ministry seminars, and whatever else you can do to train yourself. It may feel selfish, but honestly it'll allow you to put so much more back into the ministry. It also will give you a sense of hope, confidence, and direction.

As much as possible, plan the budget so that leaders can go on trips and events for free, because adult youth leaders should always go for free. (More on this in the next section.)

## Tip #3: Plan out expenses for each month.

If you only plan an annual budget, that's a good start, but make sure you designate certain funds in each category for each month of the year so you don't hit August and realize you're out of funds until January.

## Tip #4: Keep it flexible.

For me, the trick has always been to make the budget categories specific enough that expenses clearly have a label, but flexible enough that if I run out of cash in one category I can still fit items into another. Here's a breakdown of my budget's categories:

- Local outreach (local community network of youth pastors, service projects)
- Food, drinks, serving supplies, lunch with teens
- Volunteer appreciation
- Training (conferences, books)
- Graduation gifts (seriously, I can't personally afford graduation gifts for every senior every year)
- Curriculum, resources, teaching aids
- Promotions (supplies, website, communication)
- Special events (retreats, mission trips)

## Tip #5: Plan for an income.

Most youth ministries take in an income when they do significant events like a student conference or missions trip. Don't forget to take that into consideration as you put your budget together.

For example, let's say that I estimate that our trip to a student conference is going to cost us $3,000 total. I put that number in the budget, but I also make a notation that I expect $2,200 to come in from teens paying for the trip. That leaves $800 that has to cover the cost of the adult leaders. Why not just put $800 in the budget and leave it at that? Because very rarely will your actual cost be spot on $3,000 or your income be exactly $2,200. If one of those numbers is different, your budgeted money will obviously not be exactly $800, meaning you'll have to compensate appropriately. Having a rough estimate to work with at the beginning of the year can help you make sure the funds are flexible by the time the conference comes around—because you planned ahead for it.

## Tip #6: Prioritize the funds.

To make sure you don't spend budget money on something that's not very important only to find out later that you don't have money left for what's critical, assign a priority value to each of your categories. In my case, I rank food, volunteer appreciation, and training all as high priority; resources and teaching aids as medium priority; and local outreach, graduation gifts and promotions as low priority.

## Tip #7: Run it by a few adult youth leaders.

Your youth leaders are serving in this ministry with you, so let a few of them look it over and see what they think. Do they recommend you cut back in one category to add to another? Do they remember an event you need to plan for that was accidentally left out?

By the way, if they tell you to pull some money out of the volunteer appreciation category, tell them, "No way!" and explain that without them, nothing else could take place.

## Tip #8: Be careful about mixing your own finances.

Many churches handle expenses by reimbursing people after they've made the purchase from their own pocket, but I feel very strongly against that. I'm not the bankroll for youth expenses—the church's finances don't have to run through my own.

It's not a big deal for a church to get a debit card for youth expenses. In fact, it's less paperwork in the long run and it leaves my personal finances intact. The exception, unfortunately, is for my volunteer youth leaders. Since it's not prudent to give each of them a youth debit card, expenses they incur are submitted for reimbursement.

As a prospective youth pastor, this issue was actually a prerequisite of mine as I was interviewing for youth ministry jobs several years ago. My personal finances remain my own. I don't keep extra cash in my checking account just to fund youth group purchases, nor will I ever take out a personal credit card for youth expenses—even if the church promises to pay it every month. It's too risky to have that line of credit in my name in case something happens to go sour with the church.

## Other Voices

**Justin Ross:**
I do have a church credit card. When the church first gave it to me, I was almost scared to use it—especially since my wife and I don't have or want a single credit card in our name. It's been a great tool, though. I reconcile the statement with my receipts once a month and the church pays off the card. With a church debit card, I would have to do this once a week. I remember each time I swipe that card that I am spending God's money. If you have problems with debt, or if you don't trust yourself to walk by the Xbox games at Wal-Mart without deciding that you need to charge that new game "for ministry purposes," this setup is probably not for you.

# why volunteers should always go for free

Dacia Bryan, youth pastor at Higher Ground Pentecostal Holiness Church in Ahoskie, N.C., once asked me:

> "Should a portion of the money we raise go to help pay for hotel expenses for youth staff members who go with us on overnight trips? Most of my youth staff are college-age or a little older, most of them are relatively low income, and it's a pretty big sacrifice for them to take off work and chaperone trips throughout the year."

Here's my answer: Youth volunteers should never pay a dime for anything ministry-related, regardless of their income. They're already sacrificing their family time, work time, relax time, friend time, sleep, energy, and so on—that's payment enough. I try to make it easy for the leaders to go on trips—because if they can't go, neither can the teens.

I suggest splitting all the youth leaders' fees between the teens going on the trip: the cost of the trip for everyone divided by the number of teens attending. For example, if a trip costs $50/person and there are ten teens going and four leaders, I take $50×14=$700 and divide that by the ten teens, so now the trip costs $70/teen and leaders go free.

Besides making it easier for the volunteers, it shows them that you appreciate their sacrifice and dedication to the teens. Even if a leader wants to pay, don't let them. That way there's absolutely no pressure on any other leader to pay also. If some leader demands that they make some sort of financial contribution, ask them to sponsor one of the teens instead.

Now, I don't make this formula public to everyone when announcing the cost of trips and events. I just tell them what it costs and leave it at that, especially if no one is used to the slightly inflated prices. If someone asks, tell them the truth and publicly support your volunteers 100 percent. Make it clear that if the leaders don't go, then no one can go at all. Your leaders are the ones who make the trip possible for everyone—the ones sacrificing so much personally and giving so much to the teenagers during that time. The least the teens can do is cover the cost to get them there.

Unfortunately some parents have the expectation that programs should either be free of charge or offered at minimal cost. Often those same parents have no problem forking over $200 for a band uniform or paying for their teen's sports leagues. They consider those programs to be valuable. What we need to emphasize is how much more valuable their teenagers' spiritual development is.

In most cases, raising the price a little won't affect anyone— as much as any outcry may indicate otherwise. Every marketing study out there shows that teens are the number one targeted demographic because they spend more money than anyone else and have the least amount of financial responsibility. The question isn't usually whether teens have money or not—the question is how they choose to spend it. If they'd stay home one Friday night instead of going out to eat and seeing a movie with friends, that's an extra $20 right there. When my students commit to support one of our church's missionaries, it's like pulling teeth to get them to meet their $30 pledge every month. But if I announce something about paintball, every teen immediately has $40 and is ready to go.

Don't ask the leaders to pay for anything. Cover their gas, meals, lodging, and 100 percent of any other youth ministry-related expenses. Charge the teens a little extra to cover it. Give each of your leaders a hug for making the trip possible and let them know just how much you appreciate their sacrifice and dedication to the students.

## Other Voices

**Lynn Mills:**

I totally agree with the leaders going for free for the reasons stated and also that having to pay for two people out of the same household can get costly. The problem with your formula is that if you have a small youth group—say only two teenagers going—you can't split the leaders' cost because it would double their cost. I have the church pay for the youth leaders when that happens.

# investing in volunteers

A look at any ministry's budget will show where the ministry's true values lie. As you prepare your ministry's budget, make sure you invest in the volunteers. Not only should they not pay for their ministry involvement, but the budget should generously invest in them, as well.

The best investment the youth budget can make is not to buy curriculum, big promotional banners, or even to purchase Bibles. The best use of budget money is to invest in the volunteers with training and appreciation gifts. The youth ministry can't function without the volunteers. The leaders in my ministry are serving students spiritually and emotionally just as much as I am. There's no greater gift I can give teens than well-trained, passionate volunteers.

Curriculum and promotional materials may be necessary, but they won't ever leave the lasting impression on a hurting teen that care from a volunteer will. An unused Bible will never change a life for Christ, but the Holy Spirit working through an effective volunteer who encourages a teen to start reading Scripture will change a life forever.

So train your volunteers well—both in-house and with outside seminars—and then shower them with gifts and appreciation. Let them know they're valued. It doesn't have to be anything big: two movie passes for the volunteer and her spouse and free babysitting from a teen communicates, "You put so much time and energy into these teens—go relax and have a good time with your spouse." A valued and trained team is a happy and effective team, which leads to longevity in ministry.

## Other Voices

**Jason Sansbury:**

At my last church, we were blessed to be able to take the whole team to the National Youth Workers Convention. I was always amazed at how much it energized us as a team and stretched our thinking. I completely agree with you.

**Chris Day:**

This is so true. The more we invest in our leaders the more they want to invest personally and spiritually. I always put in a chunk of money for "leader development," a.k.a. me winning brownie points with our leaders. One small thing we do is buy them activity tickets for all of the high school events for the year so they don't have to pay out of pocket to support our students.

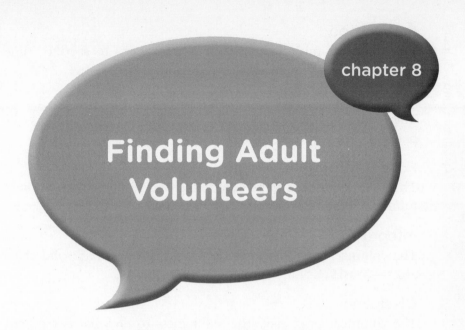

chapter 8

# Finding Adult Volunteers

## what to look for in a youth leader

Most paid youth workers know they need to put together a team of adult leaders to serve the teens and the ministry, but surprisingly few actually know what they're looking for other than someone who's breathing. Sometimes it feels as though anyone will qualify to be a youth leader as long as he's out of high school and attending the church.

While you'll never have a perfect person serve on the team, there are several important qualities you should look for when recruiting leaders:

### Growth
First and foremost, there needs to be a hunger for personal and spiritual growth. We can't lead where we haven't been. Look for someone who'll be a positive spiritual role model for teens.

### Positive attitude
The volunteer must have the ability to work well with others, and he must be able to see people and situations in a constructive way. Nothing destroys a team's momentum more quickly than someone who's negative.

## Servanthood

The volunteer must demonstrate a willingness to sacrifice time and energy for others without needing anyone to notice.

## Team player

The volunteer must have a mindset of looking out for the well-being of others and lifting others up.

## Follow-through

The volunteer needs to be committed and responsible—he must fulfill any specific ministries or jobs he takes on.

## Integrity

The volunteer must demonstrate trustworthiness and solid character—consistency in words and walk is key.

## Discipline

The volunteer must have the willingness to do what is required regardless of mood. This is someone who understands that youth meetings and events are for students, and thus he has the discipline to stay student-minded regardless of how he feels in the moment or in light of any distractions that may come.

## Relational

The volunteer must have the ability to make others feel comfortable. Every teen matters and needs to be known, greeted, and cared for.

## Sense of humor

The volunteer must have the ability to laugh at himself, try new things, and have a good time learning from his (and his youth pastor's) mistakes!

## Patience

The volunteer needs to be someone who is patient with himself and with others and doesn't become stressed when the learning curve is high. Look for someone who's willing to learn. He must also be patient with others, remembering that everyone is at a different place. Youth leaders need to reach out and love people where they are. Feeling comfortable and connecting with teens takes time—going to camps, retreats, and special events will help intensify and solidify relationships with teens. The more the youth leader invests, the more he'll get out of the experience, so find someone who can take initiative.

## Teachable spirit

This person needs to have the ability to be humble, open to loving criticism, and able to learn from others.

As we recruit other youth leaders, it's easy to hold a list like this against them to evaluate whether or not they match up to all these qualities, but it's also a good idea to take a look at yourself: How many of these qualities do you possess? Which ones do you need to work on to become a better leader for your ministry?

## Other Voices

**David Schmoyer:**
I like this post, although I would say people with these qualities are often approached and asked by churches to be youth leaders because they have these qualities and church leadership thinks they would work well with youth. I think in addition the person recruited needs to have the desire or passion to work with youth. I work as a nurse, and I can tell immediately if another staff member is there because he has passion for the job, or if he's there because of someone else.

**Brandon Johns:**
You forgot "the ability to consume large amounts of pizza in a single night!"

# how to recruit ministry volunteers

## What not to do:

**1. Never stand in front of your congregation and make a plea for help.**
Don't ask for anyone who might be interested to contact you. You may get a response from someone, but she could be an immature believer, have disqualifying personal issues, or sign up just to have fun. And since she knows you're in need of help, it's hard to communicate, "Sorry, we do need help, but you're not what we want." If you make a public plea, you almost have to take whoever shows up at your office door.

**2. Never beg people to join your ministry.**
You don't want people to join you out of pity, or because they have a hard time saying no. Don't come across as a ministry that's struggling and needs help in order to function. That's not very inspiring and sets a completely wrong perspective for that potential volunteer, especially if later she decides to come on board. And if some-

one joins you because she feels sorry for you, she probably won't stay long or be very committed.

**3. Never invite someone to join your ministry team unless you're confident in that person's ability to fulfill the roles you agree upon.**

Don't set your volunteer up for failure by saying, "Let's see how well you can perform here," and then later say, "Wow, I didn't know you were so bad at this. Oh well, thanks anyway!" This is a disservice to your youth group as well as to your now ex-volunteer. Set her up to succeed from the beginning.

## What to do:

**1. Ask your church staff and other trusted leaders for referrals of people they think would be a great fit for your ministry.**

Also, intentionally establish relationships with people outside of your ministry area and get a feel for where they are spiritually and how they may or may not fit into your team. Pray over every lead.

**2. Speak with other people who know the prospective volunteer.**

What input do they have? Any concerns? Can they envision that person successfully participating in your ministry?

**3. If everything checks out, approach the recruit and cast the vision for your ministry.**

Share what God's doing in your team and where you believe he's leading. Also listen to the volunteer's heart, talk about her passions and what God's doing in her life—especially points that may intersect with what God's doing in your ministry. Throughout the discussion, work to generate excitement within this potential volunteer if it looks like a good connection could be made between her and your ministry.

**4. Invite the recruit to become a part of the ministry as a fly on the wall—no responsibilities, just to observe.**

It can be intimidating for someone new to jump in with both feet when they've never been a part of a youth meeting or event before. Let her chill in the background of a couple of meetings just to observe the atmosphere, see the teenagers, hear the stories, and experience it for herself. Then debrief.

**5. If the volunteer agrees to join the ministry, set clear expectations and responsibilities.**

Provide ongoing training and support as the volunteer ventures out into her specific area of ministry. This ensures that she won't burn out right away and will be a part of your group for a long time to come. Also make sure you take care of any legal stuff your church might require, including background checks and application process.

### 6. Set your standards high and keep 'em there!

The last thing your ministry needs is a questioned reputation because someone on your team did something or said something that was stupid or downright harmful. Your ministry should always be a safe place where people have full confidence in the integrity of your volunteers.

## Other Voices

### Justin Ross:

Beyond my youth ministry volunteer team, I also recruit others to help with our special events. A couple of weeks ago, I approached an elder in our church about helping. He doesn't have a heart for working in youth ministry, but I don't need someone with a heart for youth ministry to grill hamburgers. He was glad to do that. This way, I keep youth events in front of others in the congregation who would never be involved otherwise, and my youth ministry volunteers and I get to spend our time with teens.

### Benjer McVeigh:

I invite our current team to take part in the recruiting process. If I've done a good job communicating to our team the mission and vision of the ministry as well as the expectations of leaders, they'll be in a great position to recommend good potential leaders.

## addressing the four most common excuses potential leaders make

In the spring of 2007, the ratio of leaders to students in my ministry was about 1 to 10, which was way too high for us—so we started recruiting leaders. We recruited by approaching individuals we knew who possessed the qualities we were looking for in an adult role model, casting the vision for our ministry, and asking them to consider joining us.

We were met with several excuses. Here are the top four we encountered and ideas for how to respond to them:

# 1. I just don't have the time.

People make time for the things they count as important. Share with the potential leader the importance of leadership in the body of Christ—cast a vision for life-change that can occur for students in youth ministry.

# 2. I don't have the gift of leadership.

Remember that leadership is mostly character. If you believe an adult has the basic character qualities of a potential leader, remind him that he'll get the training he needs to be effective (but only say that if you'll really follow through with training him, of course).

# 3. I'm not the leadership type.

At this point you need to explore what the person means by leadership type. Perhaps he has a definition of leadership that's not biblical. Perhaps he views a leader as someone who's in charge and in control, as opposed to someone who can facilitate life change by caring for, shepherding, discipling, and loving others.

# 4. I'm too old.

There's no such thing as "too old" for youth ministry. We'll address this one in depth in the next section.

## Other Voices

**Tony Myles:**

There are several types of youth workers, but most people tend to think of only one version: the stereotypical young youth worker who leads teens with an abundance of charisma and adrenaline. There are other ways to lead that involve influence that comes from age, relationships, spiritual maturity, biblical authority, and so on. As you recruit, don't attempt to attract just one type of youth worker—do your best to cast a vision for how anyone can impact teenagers if that person loves God and loves teens.

**Aaron Giesler:**

When I recruit leaders I try to match people with their gifting. When the potential leaders see I have their success in mind, they tend to be more willing to serve in the ministry.

**Lars Rood:**

I think the reason people make excuses is that we've done a poor job of talking about needs and leadership roles that can fit many people. In our group we have a handout that starts with a statement, "Can you give one hour?" and it has jobs that would serve the youth ministry if someone only had one hour a week. Then it goes up from there. We try to block those excuses before they happen by making sure we have jobs for people who have little time, don't feel like they're leaders, or don't know what their gifts are.

## the value of using retired adults

It seems like most youth pastors and senior pastors think that college students or young married couples make the best youth workers. This is usually because "The teens can relate to them" or "They're energetic."

Looking back over my 10 years in youth ministry, I can honestly say that I've had more challenges with college students and young married couples than any other volunteer demographic. Granted, I fit into the "young married" category myself right now, so I'm not criticizing that age group—it's just that every single retired youth worker I've had was absolutely wonderful.

Here's why you should consider recruiting youth workers from the retirees in your church:

### Life experience
They have the life experience and wisdom no young adult or college student could ever have. They've been through the school of hard knocks, they've learned valuable life lessons, they know what it's like to make both good and bad decisions, and they're usually more than willing to share that wisdom with others.

### Spiritual maturity
Oftentimes retired people are the prayer warriors of your church. They're the ones who love to tell people about Christ and what he's done in their lives. They love the Lord with all their heart and have a relationship with him that's contagious to those around them.

### Love teens
Many retired people are grandparents and love teenagers. Many of the teenagers in your youth group love their grandparents, too. But what if their grandparents live too far away or are in heaven now? There's potential for the retired adults to become "grandma" and "grandpa" to those teens. Plus, this older demographic has already raised their own children and has had years of experience with teens.

## Time available

It may be hard for college students and young professionals to invest time in teens because of jobs, family, and everything else going on. Many retired couples have more time to invest in teens throughout the week and love spending their time with teenagers.

## Incredible role models

Many retired Christian adults live lives outside the youth ministry and church that are consistent with what they say and do inside the church. These adults can provide living examples for teenagers that lifelong marriages are possible, that faith intersects life every day, and that imitating Christ is both possible and incredible.

Most retired adults and senior citizens are surprised when I approach them with the idea of serving in the youth ministry. The first excuse is, "Oh, I'm too old for that. I don't know anything about modern teenagers." My response is always to reassure them that it's okay. "Teenagers don't care if you know all the latest bands, have seen the top movie of the season, or if you can play dodge-ball. All they want to know is that you love them and that you care about them." Then I run through some of the reasons why I think they'd make great youth leaders and share how they can become irreplaceable partners in the vision for our youth ministry.

## Other Voices

**Corey Potter:**
I recently came through a youth group and I currently help out as a leader in the youth group. I know that as a teen I would have felt awkward with a retired adult as a youth volunteer. I think teens do care about whether or not they feel comfortable with the leaders, and especially in our church, the teens aren't very comfortable with the older adults. It might be because the older adults are very traditional and the youth have had bad experiences with them. I feel like the teenagers in our youth group would have a hard time being themselves because they would feel like the adults were always watching them. And they would feel awkward because the retired adults don't like the same things the teens do. I also think they'd probably get the, "You're too old to understand—things were different when you were young" attitude from our teens. Maybe this is just our church, but I feel like it wouldn't go over well.

**Tim's response to Corey:**

Point well taken. However, it sounds to me that it's an issue of stereotypes rather than an "old person" issue. I think the teens might feel that way at first, but what if the retired adult truly demonstrated to the teenagers how much he cares for them and that he's there to listen and encourage them—not to judge or be critical? I'm sure the teens could quickly change their minds if that's the genuine heart of the older adult. If it's not, then yes, you're absolutely correct, but you shouldn't recruit adults who don't have a heart for teens, regardless of their age.

**Shan Smith:**

I have an 83-year-old gentleman who helps in the youth ministry, and the teenagers love him. They say, "He's the coolest old guy I know."

**Justin Ross:**

Invite the oldest people in your congregation to come to youth group and talk about what their church looked like when they were teenagers. Ask things such as: "What did your youth ministry look like?" "How seriously did teens take their faith?" "What did you struggle with?" and "What sins did you see as most dangerous?" It's amazing to hear stories like this and realize that while we live in a completely different world than they did 50 or 60 years ago, much has remained the same.

## should you use unsaved adults as youth leaders?

A friend of mine serves in a church youth ministry of about 150 teens, many of whom are from the community and don't know Christ. At a recent parent meeting, a couple of unsaved parents asked him about helping out at youth meetings. This led to the question: Can nonbelieving parents be "staff" on youth nights and trips as long as they aren't put in a teaching position? Is it okay to use non-Christian parents to help oversee the game room, serve concessions, and greet teens as they arrive and leave? At least then they would be exposed to the gospel. Maybe they would give their lives to Christ along with their teens, right?

Personally, I don't think it's a wise move. I wouldn't let unsaved parents serve in my ministry for many reasons. Here are three:

### 1. Whether I like it or not, youth workers become role models for the teenagers.

I wouldn't put any unsaved adult in that position for my teens. I won't even put a new believer or any emotionally or spiritually immature person in that role, either. It doesn't matter if that person is a teacher or a server—teens will still see them as an authority figure. The new teen who visits will have no idea that this adult they're watching isn't intended to be a role model. And there's no way an unsaved adult can be a spiritual role model.

### 2. Even if an unsaved youth worker is well intentioned, she won't share the same values and goals I do as a Christian.

We won't even think on the same wavelength. The last thing we need is an adult making unwise statements or actions toward a teen. An unsaved adult is at a much higher risk for this to happen.

### 3. Youth group is not intended to be the place for evangelism to adults.

The primary ministry of youth group is to the teenagers. They come first. If I were in this situation, I'd encourage those parents to get involved in other areas of the church that are geared specifically for them. Or, I'd go hang out at their house for dinner with the family sometime and share the gospel then.

## Other Voices

**Mike Ferber:**
I think there's a clear distinction between "staff" and "parents." I would strongly encourage parents to get involved in activities such as concessions or making sure teens don't kill each other in the game room. However, I would not classify them as "staff." That's a key distinction.

**Tim's reply to Mike:**
I don't see any distinction between parents and staff at all. Practically speaking, I don't think teens do, either. This is especially true of visitors, who don't know people and will have a harder time telling the difference between someone they can look up to and someone they can't.

**Shane Vander Hart's reply to Mike:**
I somewhat agree with Mike. If it weren't parents who asked, I wouldn't even consider it. That being said, I understand the con-

cerns that you shared, Tim. I think what I would do is to find behind-the-scenes work for them to do. If you have a bunch of unchurched teenagers coming to your ministry, you'll have to engage with their parents at some level. That doesn't mean putting them into a position of leadership, though.

**Matt Hall:**

Inviting (allowing?) adults to have regular contact with teens does make them leaders. Students are not always aware of titles and roles or expectations—they ultimately care about relationships. Youth group should be a place of positive, Christ-based, role-model relationships.

**Justin Ross:**

I have several teenagers who come from families who don't attend church at all. If any of those parents asked me about coming to youth group, I would never exclude them. I don't think any of my teens have difficulty distinguishing between volunteers and visitors. (I would certainly consider the parents visitors, not volunteers.) I'm just glad they allow their child to come to my group—especially when church is not a priority or major concern for them. If they care enough to want to know what happens on Wednesday nights, they're welcome. A random person who is not a Christian who wants to hang out with teens? No way. But a parent of one of my teens is welcome. Unfortunately, this has yet to happen.

**Aaron Giesler:**

To me, it really depends on what role you're talking about. If a parent wants to be part of his child's life, then I have a hard time telling him he can't be around. Like many parents who want to get involved, I would tell him to observe for a couple of weeks before we do anything official. If that unsaved parent wants to help after seeing what we're all about, then I would say yes, but I would clearly define his role. It would be limited and not in any leadership capacity.

## the process of initiating new leaders into the ministry

It's helpful to have a laid-out plan ahead of time about how your ministry initiates new leaders into the ministry. It helps you avoid common mistakes as well as ensuring that you cover all your bases before your volunteers are welcomed as leaders and given full access to teens.

Below is the process I use for introducing new volunteers to the youth ministry at my church. There's no formula for how this needs to work—it's just what we do. Your conversations should—and will—be different from ours:

## 1. Contact the prospective youth worker.

You've expressed an interest in serving God by loving teens, but are unsure as to where you can help. We'll help you with this. Most of the time "unlikely people" make the greatest youth workers, so even if you're unsure, prayerfully consider this ministry, and we'll help you take the next step.

## 2. Conduct an initial meeting between you and the volunteer.

This is an opportunity for us to briefly connect so I can know more about your desire to be involved in ministry. We'll also give you a general overview of the ministry and arrange for you to visit and observe our programs.

## 3. Give the prospective youth leader any applicable youth ministry material.

Read over all the pages and information in the staff application. The packet gives you the basic information you'll need to help you make decisions about how you'd like to be involved in our ministry. We've tried to give you a good idea of what it's like, but you'll get a clearer picture when you observe a program.

## 4. Encourage the volunteer to look at your youth group website.

Our youth ministry is not limited only to weekly meetings and periodic events—the Internet is changing the way people work and function, especially for this younger generation. Take a look at how we connect with teens and parents online.

## 5. Encourage the prospective youth leader to observe some programs.

We encourage you to observe a program or event. This is a good opportunity to get a better feel for the ministry without having expectations and responsibilities placed on you. You'll have a chance to meet teens and other staff and write down any questions you may have for our future meeting. You may feel uncomfortable while observing a program (teens don't typically go out of their way to make you feel welcome until you get to know them), so keep that in mind.

## 6. Have the volunteer complete an application package.

This application package was developed so that we might obtain appropriate information for our screening process. This process not only protects us and protects our students, but it protects you. In the unfortunate case that false accusations are made concerning a staff member's integrity, we have this process to show that you are creditable and have a clean history. We require that all the pages in this packet be filled out and returned to the youth pastor. Please also include two references. You can choose a pastor, close friend, and/or an employer from within the last year.

## 7. Interview the prospective youth leader. (See the next section.)

This is an opportunity for you to share your thoughts from your observations of our youth group, describe your spiritual journey, and communicate your gifts and desires for working with the youth ministry. We'll also discuss your application and more specific roles you could potentially play in this ministry.

## 8. Encourage the volunteer to prayerfully consider her commitment.

We want you to take time to pray and think through your commitment. We encourage you to seek the counsel of family and/or friends regarding your commitment.

## 9. Ask the volunteer to commit to serve in youth ministry and request consent for the criminal record check.

Sign a commitment sheet and turn it in to the youth pastor along with the Consent for Criminal Record Search. Your application process does not go any further until your criminal record check is received. Don't worry, when it comes, all of your information will be kept under strict confidence.

## 10. Establish a time for the volunteer to begin ministry.

After you have committed to serve in youth ministry and we've received the criminal background check, we'll discuss a beginning date. This date will vary depending on your intended involvement.

## 11. Inform the volunteer of evaluation meetings.

At your two-month and four-month mark, we'll meet to evaluate your feelings and perceptions regarding your involvement with youth group. We'll continue to evaluate throughout the year and, if necessary, adjust your role to better fit your style, personality, and strengths.

## Other Voices

**Jason Hughlett:**

It usually seems to be the other way around for me: I have to track people down and ask if they'd like to help out and that's usually because we have a hole to fill. This means that we may not be utilizing their specific gifts, but we can always be in review mode and make sure that we don't miss out on those gifts.

# questions to ask a new youth leader

It's a good idea to interview every new youth leader before unleashing him to be a spiritual role model for teens. If you're the paid youth director, you're the one who stands between the teens and a potentially harmful adult, so be very careful with this process. Even if you know the prospective youth worker very well, still have a formal meeting where you sit down with the individual and clarify some very important issues.

Your church's insurance company may have a list of questions they want you to go through with each youth leader, so be sure to check with them if you haven't already done so. Here are some additional items I like to follow up on:

## Spirituality

- When and how did you become a Christian? List any circumstances or people that influenced you to make this decision.
- How is God working in your life now?
- How would you describe your spiritual journey and your relationship with God today? What are your struggles (we all have them!)? What's going well?
- In what ways has God used your gifts, talents, and abilities to bring glory to himself? How has that tied in with your heart for leading teens?
- How well do you know your Bible? Do you feel comfortable teaching it to others?

- How have you gained the amount of Bible knowledge that you presently possess?
- Do you have a spiritual accountability partner?
- Are you open to greater spiritual accountability?

## Past History

- Have you ever gone through treatment for alcohol or drug abuse?
- Have you ever been ticketed for reckless driving or driving under the influence?
- Have you ever been arrested, detained, or questioned by police for any other illegal actions of any type?
- Has there been alcohol abuse, drug abuse, physical abuse, or sexual abuse in your family background?
- If yes, what steps have you taken to minimize the impact that those issues will create for you, both now and in the future?
- Have you ever been treated for any type of psychiatric disorder?
- Have you ever been accused, charged, or alleged to have committed any act of neglect, abuse, or molestation of any child?
- Is there any circumstance or pattern in your life that would make it inappropriate for you to serve with minors or would compromise the integrity of our church?
- Do you have any communicable diseases we should be aware of?
- Are you under medication or treatment for any disease or condition we should be aware of?

## Ministry

- How do you decide which movies are acceptable for you to view?
- Would you feel comfortable recommending all of your music to a teen? Why or why not?
- Please list the dates and activities of other ministry experiences that you have been involved in here at our church.
- What is your personal vision for ministry at our church? Do you have any ideas of how God might accomplish that through you?
- Why would you like to join the youth volunteer leadership team?
- Is there anything else you feel we need to know about you?

Please note that none of the answers to these questions will necessarily eliminate someone from serving in our youth ministry. They're just here to open the dialogue and make sure we bring up the issues.

The following is also part of our process of recruiting youth volunteers:

## Prayer Partners

We also ask each youth leader to find five prayer partners. These are other adults who'll commit to praying for the volunteer on a regular basis regarding her ministry with the teenagers. The youth leader must turn in her prayer partners' names and contact info to me so I can add them to our ministry's prayer mailing list.

## References

Each youth leader also submits two references whom we either call and interview, or we ask these references to fill out a questionnaire about the prospective youth leader. While it may feel like more paperwork, it's absolutely critical. Have an honest conversation about the potential youth leader and the access she'll have to minors.

## Background Checks

Do it! No exceptions. No excuses. Make sure the church has a background check on file for you, too. Having worked in two churches where youth leaders were taken to court for inappropriate sexual conduct with youth (one went to prison, the other didn't), I know just how critical this is. No one is immune, nor is anyone an exception. Do it now before it's too late! Seriously. Do it.

Some have said that this process of interviewing leaders, setting boundaries and expectations is too rigorous. They say, "We're just thankful to get people to work with the youth! This process is an obstacle—no one will take the time to be so scrutinized."

My response: It's absolutely an obstacle . . . and one that's totally necessary. If a potential youth leader is either too apathetic to go through the process, or is nervous about being scrutinized, then I don't want that person on the team in the first place.

Anyone passionate about teens will be willing to go through this process and will see the value in being cautious about which adult leaders are officially established as spiritual influences and which ones aren't.

## Other Voices

**D.J. Butcher:**

For background checks, I agree that they need to be done. However, they get really pricey! I know of one particular megachurch that doesn't even do them, but instead reserves the right to. They just don't advertise that they don't do it. I think that's pretty wise. If you take the information and let possible volunteers know that you're taking information for a background check, that will serve as a deterrent as well. And then you have the option to do certain checks on individuals you may feel unsure of.

**Tim's reply to D.J.:**

Background checks can be pricey—but they're worth every penny. My previous church also just collected the information and never followed through. The problem with that is if there's something on a leader's record, you'll never know! The $25 to have someone screened is absolutely worth the teens' safety. It's much cheaper than the legal fees that could come later. The only reason that church isn't following through is because they haven't been scared enough to see how big of a deal this really is, and if they ever are scared enough (God forbid!) it will be too late.

# what teens need from youth leaders

Changing the world happens one teen at a time—not in bulk at big events. This is because—as we've said before—teens don't connect with programs; instead, they connect with people. The most effective way teens are influenced is by significant relationships with key people in their lives. Our goal is to develop adult youth leaders who will minister to teens on a personal level.

The teenagers in our youth groups need adult leaders who will—

- Grow spiritually on a personal level and let Jesus live through them.
- Be interested in their lives.
- Take the initiative to spend time with them.
- Pray for them.
- Be real.
- Speak encouraging words.
- Believe in them.
- Laugh with them.

- Go to "their world."
- Remember their names and care for them.
- Share God's love with them.
- Be consistent in life and ministry.
- Be patient.
- Enjoy life and help teens enjoy life.
- Be a leader for teenagers, not a peer.

## Other Voices

### Brandon Johns:

Bring them into your world from time to time (take them shopping or ask for their help running errands).

### Brian Ford:

Help them walk through the tough questions about life. And when we don't have an answer, admit we don't know but we're certainly going to try our best using God's Word to find the right answer. Then keep that promise and get back to them.

### Mike Kupferer:

Model integrity and humility.

### Justin Ross:

Ask how you can pray for them that week—and then do it. The next week, follow up with them. Show them that you not only cared enough to ask, but that you also followed through.

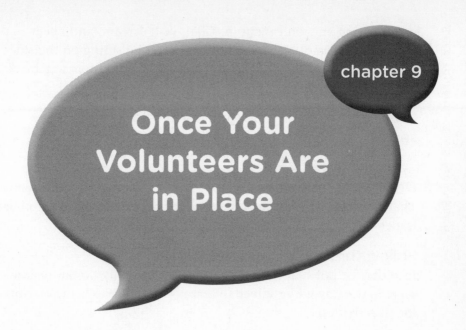

# chapter 9

# Once Your Volunteers Are in Place

## expectations of youth leaders

I'm not sure there can ever be a complete list of expectations for adult youth leaders. Every ministry has different expectations for people who play different roles and carry different levels of responsibility. The following list is what I use as a starting point with the volunteer youth workers at my church:

### Be committed to God and to the student ministry at our church.

Regularly attend church services, participate in worship, and commit to tithing.

### Mingle with teens from any school and make newcomers feel welcome.

New people will feel out of place, so the more people who say hi and learn their names the better. This doesn't mean that you have to spend hours with them, but let them know they're noticed. Don't forget to say hello the next week, too. Remember their names. And remember that everyone is welcome no matter what he looks like, smells like, or how he talks.

### Participate wholeheartedly.

Any game can be fun if you want it to be. Be the first to jump up when it's time to get in a team or a line, etc. Look for people not participating and pull them in. Clap, yell, scream, and cheer . . . when appropriate. No youth leader should be sitting on the sidelines. Watch for people cheating, and if the game starts to break down, seek to correct it.

### If you're in a boyfriend/girlfriend relationship, stay sexually pure and continue to be above reproach.
Set an excellent standard in all that you do.

### Dress very modestly.
The last thing we want is to be a subject of lust to teens or other leaders.

### Follow through on responsibilities.
In order for our team to work together smoothly, we all need to serve in the way we've agreed to serve. This includes being on time for all activities.

### If you're driving students anywhere, seatbelts and speed limits are a must.
The law is the law and it's there to help keep us safe. Even if you're late and the seatbelts are uncomfortable, you must abide by the law at all times, model good citizenship for the teenagers, and take precautions to keep the teens safe.

### Pray regularly for the youth ministry and its leaders.
Pray for the teens, the ministry, the other leaders, your pastors, yourself, your church, your community, and for everything else that surrounds the youth ministry. Without the Holy Spirit working in your ministry, no life-change will take place, so beg the Holy Spirit to join you in every way possible.

### If you have a concern about anything involving the teenagers you work with or the youth ministry, contact the youth pastor immediately.
It's important that you do this before chatting about the situation with another leader, parent, or teen—that's gossip, which can lead to a host of other problems. Even when the problem is with the youth pastor, take the high road and speak with him directly. And if someone else comes to you with an issue she hasn't yet shared with the youth pastor, don't entertain her concerns until she's talked to the appropriate people first.

It's very important that you let the youth pastor know beforehand if you're unable to attend an event.
This is especially true if you're leading any specific part of the event. Please make arrangements so any responsibilities under your care are properly addressed.

## Attend staff trainings and meetings.
It's important not only for your personal development as a youth leader, but also for building unity as a team of youth leaders who've joined forces to reach a community of teens for Christ.

## Commit to regular prayer, Bible study, evangelism, personal worship, Scripture memorization, and accountability.
You have to be growing yourself before you can expect to help teenagers do it. And you can't teach students to practice something you don't practice yourself. Become someone who demonstrates a life of spiritual growth for teens.

## Find areas of need in the youth ministry and offer suggestions for improvement.
It's easy to find areas that need work, because every ministry has them. It's even easier to be critical about them, which is fine if done in a way that demonstrates love and humility. But make sure to focus on solutions that will help the ministry move forward in those areas.

## Commit to the vision.
Whatever the vision is for the teens in your church, every youth leader needs to be committed to advancing it, shaping it, and fleshing it out within the context of your ministry. No team works well when its members are going in different directions—nothing will destroy progress more than a disunited team.

## Maintain your public witness in private and online as well as in public.
As youth leaders, we're spiritual role models. And whether they're aware of it or not, teens are watching us very carefully.

## Other Voices

### Kevin Twombly:
Setting these expectations up front is key to having great leaders. It can also keep you from the frustration caused by a leader

not doing what's expected of him. I've heard people voice frustrations about youth leaders, and my first question is whether they've established any expectations. Usually the frustrated ones have not.

**Shan Smith:**

It's important to remember that the expectations you set for yourself shouldn't necessarily be the expectations you communicate to your volunteers. Because I'm so driven with such high self-expectations, I've lost some good volunteers because they felt they must maintain the passion, speed, and drive that I've communicated through my actions. I've had resignation conversations with good volunteers because I didn't communicate that I never expected them to invest in the same way I do. I agree with Kevin: We need to communicate expectations frequently.

## boundaries for youth leaders

Boundaries are critical for the health of any youth leader. We could talk about the need to say no in order to protect personal and family time. We could talk about setting emotional boundaries. We could also talk about setting boundaries on how vulnerable we make ourselves with teenagers (such as sharing details about a divorce or addiction). But many of those topics have been discussed at length in other books, so let's talk about some other boundaries that may be understood but never explicitly stated until it's too late.

We must utilize careful judgment at all times in the exercise of personal freedom—particularly when associating with and/or relating to teens, either publicly or privately. We recognize that many of us have opinions and practices that differ from one another, and furthermore, the Bible isn't explicit about every issue within our culture. Nevertheless, many Christians have different opinions about what behavior and practices are not acceptable for believers, so we do our best to honor those differences in order to not become a stumbling block for anyone (Romans 14:13, Luke 17:2).

Lifestyle issues are further complicated by the reality that in youth ministry we're in a position of trust and influence. Therefore—with respect to such issues as the use of language, entertainment, gambling, and other behavioral matters that are open to abuse, misuse, or misunderstanding—keep in mind the following biblical principles:

- The Bible condemns self-indulgence while commanding self-control (Galatians 5:19-25).
- The Bible commands respect of one's body (1 Thessalonians 4:4, 1 Corinthians 6:18-20).
- Community interests are to be put ahead of self-interest (Philippians 2:3-5).

Personal liberty is to be set aside—

- When its exercise could hinder a teen's spiritual development.
- When its exercise could be misunderstood in such a way as to hinder one's own witness, or that of our student ministry.
- When culture suggests the need for Christian leaders to exercise self-restraint.
- When an action could endanger another person's safety or well-being.

The following list is of boundaries I hold for myself and other adult leaders who serve in the youth ministry at my church. This is not intended to be a legalistic definition of right and wrong— instead it's meant to provide principles that will keep us accountable because of the position of influence in which we find ourselves:

- No driving girls alone in your car if you're a guy and no driving guys alone in your car if you're a girl—ever! It's not acceptable and there's no exception. Sometimes there are sticky situations that may seem unavoidable, but they are avoidable. Call someone, get help, make two trips, be honest, and do whatever it takes to avoid the situation. This sets parents' minds at ease, protects the ministry's reputation, and protects you. Along these same lines, be careful about even being alone in a room at church for too long with a student of the opposite gender.
- No dating youth members. Staff/student romantic relationships are an absolute no. Even if the romantic attention a teen gives you is flattering, have nothing to do with it.
- Female youth leaders will work best with teenage girls and male leaders will work best with the teenage guys. Mingling with the opposite sex is great, but make an attempt to maintain focus on teens of your gender.
- Dating a fellow youth staff member is no problem (unless you're married), but please keep your focus on the teens at

youth group. No PDA. If you're married, then PDA with your spouse is fine, but keep it under control. Whether we like it or not, teens are watching us very closely. Some of them may not see a healthy marriage modeled for them at home, so feel free to give them glimpses into your marriage relationship— but always keep it clean and keep it Christ-centered.

- No swearing permitted. In no way can foul language be promoted. This includes coarse joking, rude remarks, gossip, inappropriate sarcasm, and negativity.

## Other Voices

### Brian Kirk:

"No driving girls alone in your car if you're a guy and no driving guys alone in your car if you're a girl—ever!" Tim, I agree with this and would go a step further: No driving girls alone if you're a girl. No driving guys alone if you're a guy. My ministries utilize a two-adult rule (as do the Boy Scouts and others), which states that at least two adults must be present with youth in any situation. Simply ruling against opposite sex one-on-one situations doesn't account for the fact that you possibly have gay youth in your ministry, or gay adults. The two-adult rule accounts for any issues.

### Tim's reply to Brian:

I agree with you . . . mostly. If there are two adults available, I definitely recommend that both be present. However, I think it's becoming too easy for churches to start crippling ministry out of fear of what could happen. There's risk no matter what. The risk is greatly minimized by not allowing opposite sex students and leaders to be alone together, but when you say I can't ever talk to a teen alone, I feel like it's slipping into the crippling-the-ministry-too-much area. I feel comfortable taking the risk of driving a guy home once in a while if necessary.

### Justin Ross:

At the local high school, teachers are almost always part of a union who protect them and their jobs if students ever make allegations. This gives time for an investigation and for the truth to be made known. As youth workers, we don't have a union. Some denominations may offer very limited protection, but that's a situation in which none of us wants to ever find himself. Paul's words to young Timothy about leaders always being above reproach in 1 Timothy 3:1-13 are just as true now as they were then.

# handling volunteers who are too busy for teenagers

A youth pastor who wishes to remain anonymous wrote me with the following question:

> I'm in my first year of youth ministry. . . . My biggest headache has been that all of my volunteers—including my wife—are super busy and they don't have much time to really invest in these teens. We don't have a huge youth group (20 or so), but I can't invest in them all or I'll just be another statistic. Some have said, "If your volunteers don't have time then they shouldn't be youth leaders." But if I do that then I won't have anybody. I have teenagers who're excited about the Lord and ready to go, but my people don't have the time to minister to them well. I can do it with some, but not with all. Do you have some thoughts?

I'm sure he's not alone. Any youth pastor who has volunteers probably wishes those leaders would spend more time with the teens outside of church and youth group.

If you're in that position, you have a few options:

1. You can try to do it all yourself and burn out faster than belly button lint in a forest fire.
2. You can continue trying to suck more time out of your volunteers.
3. You can invest in a few teens on your own, knowing that it's better to impact a few than none at all.

As for the youth pastor who wrote me, his message indicates that he's wise enough not to do #1 and that he's already figured out that #2 doesn't work, so it sounds like #3 is the best option he has left.

If you don't have enough leaders to be able to invest in each teen individually, then you'll have to start with a few and pour your life into them. Don't worry about the critics who accuse you of playing favorites—it's better to invest in the lives of a few teenagers than in none at all.

As you set the example and invest in a few teens on your own, here are some suggestions that might help the other adults come on board with their priorities and commitments:

### Share stories with the other leaders about your time with the teens.

Tell them about the life-changes you see taking place, show them how excited you are, talk about the ways God has rewarded you and stretched you through it. In essence, make them feel like they're missing out on a huge opportunity—because they are: They're missing out on the opportunity to change lives for Christ.

### Hold a high standard for your volunteers.

Nothing communicates to a teen "you're not that important to me" more than showing them you don't have time for them. For the sake of your teens, don't let adults do that to them if you have the authority to prevent it. Ask your volunteers to commit to a higher standard, then hold them to it. It's better to have one or two committed adults than ten half-committed ones.

### Ask God to raise adult leaders in your community.

Don't just pray with the same passion most people pray with when asking God to speed up the line at the DMV—beg God for leaders, plead with him. Present your case in prayer and desperately ask God to supply role models who'll partner with you. But in the meantime, be willing to accept that his answer might be, "Right now I just want to use you in this community of teens even though you're outnumbered like Gideon."

### Lovingly challenge your volunteers' priorities.

Only you know if you have a relationship with the adults that will permit you to do this, and even if you do, make sure you talk with your senior pastor or supervisor first. Seek his advice on how to best approach this.

### Other Voices

**Terry Moore:**
#3 would clearly be the best way, and to add to it: You can train youth to reach youth. This would take time to develop, but you could be using the time of teens and in the long run you're only investing in those you're training so they might reach the others even more.

**Grant English:**
I'd suggest a fourth alternative: Create the space for volunteers to spend time with teens. Plan "hang time" every week as a part of your weekly schedule (15 minutes at the start or at the end), plan

"random" lunches where adults can eat lunch with teens at a fast food restaurant. The point is if relational hang time is important to you (and it is) then make it a part of every time you get your crew together.

**Jeremy Hallquist:**
My thought would actually be to flip the scenario around. We believe that teens need to be reached at all costs. I'm learning that sometimes our adults need to be reached as well. I'd encourage your teens to take the time to personally invite adults into their lives. Just as we do in growing the program via teens (teens reaching out to teens) sometimes the most effective tool can be the very one you're trying to grow. I know that as a volunteer I feel incredibly excited and willing to invest when I've been personally invited by a teen.

Start by asking the teens which adults they might want to have chaperone an event, and then have the teen personally seek that person out. Start small and gradually grow your volunteer base with people who become deeply committed to reaching these teens.

**Chuck Jespersen:**
I've had to learn to value my volunteers' limited time and energy. Most of my volunteers want to pour their lives into teens, but they have limits and other huge responsibilities (like family, work, home life, their own issues, and so on). What worked for us is defining what it is we want them to accomplish. We made our volunteers into small group leaders with the only expectations that they—

Lead a small group for 1.5 hours a week.
Pray for their teenagers weekly.
Write their teenagers a note each month—or build some kind of outside contact (email, attending a teen's activity, etc.).

That's all we expect from their time, and they appreciate the clear expectation—and most of them now go way beyond our expectations.

## how to train leaders to be relational

Can you identify with this youth leader?

I can't seem to get my leaders fired up about being relational with our teens. It's so frustrating. We have over 150 students in our student ministry and I'm really feeling like I'm getting to the point of burnout because of trying to connect with everyone on my own. I see the changes we need to make, but I don't feel like my leaders are ready or willing to make the necessary change. Do you have any suggestions?

Here are my suggestions for him:

## Meet with each of the leaders one-on-one (or as a couple if they're married).

Talk about their dream for youth ministry. What's their passion in youth ministry? What vision do they have for it? Why are they youth leaders? Model the relational side with them and create opportunities for them to exercise their giftedness and passion for teens. If there's no passion or love for teens, then they really have no business being volunteers. Try casting a vision with them for what you want the youth ministry to look like—make them feel a part of the process. Then, when you're discussing strategy, and relationships become a part of the conversation, they'll feel like they have ownership over it.

## Make sure leaders say no to any unrealistic expectations.

The emotional health of your volunteers is more important than the youth ministry. Besides, if they're burning out, they won't do anyone else a bit of good anyway. The best thing they can do for the teens is to protect themselves so they can continue working with teens for the long haul.

## Start the leaders off with little steps.

First, ask them to do something as simple as contact one teen a week outside of church. It only takes five or ten minutes, but that simple phone call, text message, or Facebook wall post might mean the world to a teen. After the leaders are comfortable with that, challenge them to contact every teen in their small group each week. Later, have each leader attend one teen's extracurricular game or performance during the semester. Before long, move them on to attending more teens' events. You get the idea.

Again, if volunteers are resistant to connecting with teens, I'd seriously question their reasons for working with the youth group in the first place.

## Other Voices

### Paul Bowman:

I have a great little tool for helping leaders get started on developing relationships beyond the weekly program. The 90-minute plan works well. We can't make time but we sure can take time out of our week—just 90 minutes—to really impact a life.

Consistently contact four teens each week:

- Write a Note: 10 minutes.
- Visit: 45 minutes.
- Phone: 15 minutes.
- Serve: 20 minutes (serving could be help with homework or a lift home from school—be creative).

### Mike Kupferer:

I think one of the best ways to train a volunteer to be relational is to be relational with that volunteer. Teach them to be relational with teens by modeling that kind of relationship with them. You don't have to do any extra training—just minister to them. While you're ministering to the volunteers, make sure you make comments about how you want them to spend time with teens. You shouldn't need to be blunt, but if you must, then say something like, "I want you to connect with teens in some of the same ways I've been connecting with you."

# signs that a youth leader is lacking maturity and healthy adult relationships

I know there are many signs that could be on this list, such as a youth leader needing everyone's approval, neglecting the role of the Holy Spirit, pretending to act like someone he's not, siding with teens against their parents, and so on. But there's one problem that often goes overlooked that'll undeniably create very unhealthy relationships with teens, and that's this: Every adult youth leader needs healthy adult relationships, or their relationships with students will quickly become very unhealthy.

Unfortunately, I've seen this story play out too many times. An adult youth leader may not connect well with other adults for any number of reasons: their maturity level isn't up to par, they felt rejected in high school and now try to find that security with youth group teens, they think being an adult is "un-cool," they look to teens for self-worth, and a host of other reasons that are related to emotional baggage. The result is that these volunteers become peers for teens, not leaders. And teens don't need more peers.

Here are a few signs that a youth leader is lacking maturity and healthy adult relationships:

- Whenever an issue arises in a teen's life, the leader rushes to save the day and often makes a bigger deal out of the situation than the teen does.
- When there's a disagreement between a teen and another adult youth leader, the unhealthy adult leader sides with the teen and even unintentionally pits the teen against the other leaders. This is true even in scenarios where no sides needed to be taken in the first place.
- The leader will confide in students about issues in her personal life that should only be shared with a spouse; a pastor; or a close, Christian, adult friend.
- The leader is really involved with one group of teens and generally doesn't reach out to other teenagers.
- Whenever the adult has free time, she spends most of it hanging out with the same group of teens (as a peer group) and rarely with other adult friends.
- The leader will entertain gossip and complaints (sometimes even start it) with teens about other youth leaders, the church, and even other authority figures, such as parents and teachers.
- When a teen confides in the leader, she promises to keep it a secret and never share it with anyone else. The unintentional result is that some teens who need professional help never get it. By the time you find out about it, it could be too late.
- Or a leader may take the other extreme and go out of her way to fish out juicy, private, information from teens because it strokes her ego and feeds an insecure self-worth when she knows a teen's personal secrets.
- Other adult leaders and parents whom you know and trust express concern to you about the leader (in a non-gossipy way), and their input aligns with your unspoken observations.
- When you try to express concern about any of this to the leader, she becomes defensive and makes excuses—possibly separating from the team of adult leaders even more than she already was.

Because these volunteers are lacking maturity, they'll unintentionally create division and will ultimately hinder the maturing process for teens. Often their hearts are in the right place and they mean well, but they're blinded by immaturity and fail to see the damage they're actually causing.

So, how should you handle it? Every situation is unique, but here are some general principles:

- First, it's important that you spend a decent amount of time in prayer. It's an obvious first step that too often goes overlooked.
- Talk with your senior pastor (and other church leadership, if necessary) about the situation and get their input. These conversations always work best with godly advice and guidance.
- Sit down one-on-one with the youth leader and have an honest, open conversation. Do your best to speak the truth in love. Express your concern and pray she's receptive.
- If the youth leader humbly sees truth in your observations, then work together to connect her with other maturing adults who'll help her grow spiritually, relationally, and emotionally. Establish some sort of regular, ongoing mentoring relationship—either with you or someone else.

If she makes excuses, gets defensive, and refuses to listen to your concerns, then discuss the next steps with your senior pastor. The process from here will be pretty sticky. Depending on the severity of her immaturity, there's a good chance that the youth leader may need to be asked to step down. Sometimes she can be dismissed with the intention of restoration after certain expectations have been met—such as establishing accountability, working through some personal issues, mentoring, and establishing healthy adult relationships. Other times she'll have to be dismissed permanently. Either way, the confrontation is often the most helpful component, because how a person responds to confrontation will show her true character.

Be forewarned: Dismissing this kind of a leader will be a very ugly process. The teens who love her will definitely look at you like you're the bad guy. Even though you're doing it for their benefit, you can't tell them that because then you'd have to explain why you're doing it, and you would never talk poorly about someone else just to make yourself look better (even though the other party may not play by the same rules). But you still have to do what's in the best interest of the teens and the ministry whether the teenagers understand it or not. Sometimes being a leader is like being a parent: You have to make the tough decisions for the sake of the teenagers even if they don't like it.

## Other Voices

### Benjer McVeigh:

I'm thankful that when I was hired in my first position overseeing a youth ministry right out of college, my boss said that I needed to acquire three things if I wanted to accept the position: a car, a cell phone (which they would pay for), and a Christian mentor to meet with on a regular basis. My boss was a very wise woman. I think I could have lived without the first two, but the third made me a much better youth pastor. This is great advice for any youth leader, but especially one who might be lacking in maturity.

The best way to handle this is to set guidelines up front about expectations of spiritual and emotional maturity and hold leaders to them. Not legalistic rules—clear guidelines. In addition, it's great to train leaders on these issues before they come up, and you should always model appropriate boundaries.

### Rob Gillen:

I had to walk through a process like this one nearly two years ago, and I followed all of the steps listed above. In my experience prayer and counsel from my senior pastor were the two most important. In the three months following the choice to remove this leader, I had to deal with rejection from teenagers, other youth leaders, and even parents who didn't agree with my decision. They gossiped about me and blatantly attacked me before other leaders and parents. The fallout is most heavy when you don't have longevity behind you yet.

A year later our youth group was stronger, deeper, and more intimately consumed by God than ever before. Three years later it's a lesson I've learned and history no one in our church even remembers.

Your decision to do the right thing and remove that leader (if need be) will be one of the hardest things you ever do in ministry, and it will be the decision that bears the most fruit as well.

### Gerald Faulkner:

I do see where I—in my early days—had some issues with being the adult. When my wife and I first started, we both believed the ministry was about being a friend to the teens. Wow, how stupid were we? We immediately undermined the youth director—though not intentionally. We also began having sleepovers and such at our home. In all honesty we did this not so much to be good examples, but instead so we had people to hang with.

When that high school group left, we pretty much stopped helping out with the teens: We didn't connect with the younger teens who were coming up because we had become friends with the "cool" seniors.

I'm now so glad God helped me see the difference and I'm very thankful nothing wrong ever came about through those relationships. I'm now a responsible leader and have the teens' best interests in mind—not my own. I want to be their spiritual leader first—not their friend.

# 10 ideas for keeping leaders on board long term

When I first came to my church in February of 2006, there were about 20 adult youth leaders on board. Three years later, we had 72 adults serving in one capacity or another in the youth ministry. Most of recruiting comes down to having a strong vision that compels people to become a part of a movement that's bigger than they are. Keeping them on board for the long haul involves not only the vision, but also several other key things that I do as the youth pastor.

## 1. Continually cast the vision.
The vision drives everything we do in ministry. People don't get excited about serving when we beg them to teach a Sunday school class no one else wants to teach. The leaders need to know the difference their involvement will make in the bigger picture of where your youth ministry is going, what it's doing, and what it's becoming.

## 2. Pray for them and with them.
Your ministry needs to be saturated in prayer—that includes praying for the adult leaders. Ask them how you can pray for them and their families. Whenever you're together, pray for them. When you pray alone, remember them.

### 3. Make sure everything youth leaders do with the youth group is free.

Reimburse anything ministry-related. If a volunteer takes a teen out for ice cream, if the volunteer chaperones a trip, if a volunteer drives teens to an event, reimburse it all. We even have a youth group account set up at a local grocery store where leaders can charge food if they buy it for their small group or for a class.

### 4. Provide opportunities for training.

The largest budget line item I have for our youth ministry is training. It's by far the best way we can invest money in our youth ministry. There's no substitute for a well-trained, passionate youth leader. Curriculum only lasts a few weeks, but a leader who loves what he does and feels confident and supported by the church will do it for a long time. And we all know that longevity in youth ministry is essential for effective ministry.

### 5. Shower youth leaders with gifts, notes, and praise.

Every Christmas I make sure I write a note of appreciation to every leader, and I include a little gift. Throughout the rest of the year I send random postcards and emails encouraging my volunteers, thanking them, and telling them how much of an impact they're having. In fact, I don't think I ever send an email to a youth leader—either to an individual or to a group of leaders—without thanking them.

### 6. Always publicly support youth leaders.

Not only do they need you to thank them and praise them privately, but also they need to hear you praise them publicly as well. Every year our church has a Christian Education Appreciation Sunday where we thank our youth leaders and show them off in front of the congregation.

### 7. Model the boundaries and expectations you hold for leaders.

It really helps unify the team when you all follow a common code of conduct—it shows the rest of the team that it's not just something you expect them to do, but that this youth ministry thing is something you're all in together.

### 8. Value youth leaders' input.

If you call it a team, then make sure you treat it as such. This is not a one-man show where your leaders are little followers who do your bidding. You may be the team captain, but you're all still on a team. Listen to them, include them in decisions, and listen to their criticisms and encouragement.

## 9. Delegate the authority that goes along with a responsibility.

Unfortunately, too many youth pastors put people in charge of something while retaining all the authority of the responsibility. If you put someone in charge of an event, give her full authority over that event (within reason, of course). When one of my adult leaders or a student leader is in charge of putting something together, I support her 100 percent and do whatever she asks me to do. I even let her veto me.

## 10. Utilize their passion.

Every youth pastor feels as if there are holes in their ministry they need to fill: small groups that need leaders, classes that need teachers, trips that need chaperones. While it's tempting to use leaders to make a more complete ministry, use leaders where their passions lie, not just where you feel there are gaps.

### Other Voices

**Justin Ross:**
This begins with the youth pastor. You can't expect leaders to commit for the long haul if you're looking for your next position after two school years. (Or if you're hired at a church that has had three youth pastors in the past seven years.) Let the volunteers know that you're all in this together—that you have no plans to go anywhere. When they see your commitment, you'll see them rally behind you.

# using interns

Adult youth leaders are vital to any youth ministry, but interns allow you—as the youth pastor—to step it up a notch or two in training others in youth ministry. Since interns generally have more time to commit to serving in the ministry and will be serving alongside you, there's an opportunity to develop them as leaders more intentionally than you do your group's regular adult volunteers.

Here are several suggestions for taking committed interns to the next level of youth ministry training and service.

## 1. Be careful whom you accept as an intern.

Interns are role models for your teens. Before you unleash any-one on your students, you must be confident that they'll serve as respectful, godly examples. Internships are not a loophole for let-ting graduating seniors hang out longer at youth group.

## 2. Each internship should be unique to the individual.

There shouldn't be a one-size-fits-all internship program because every intern is different and has unique gifts, passions, and minis-try focus. When I have an intern, I usually meet with him first just to find out where his heart is, what he enjoys doing, what makes him tick, what he thinks he needs from the internship, what he thinks would be most beneficial to him, and what he needs to learn most. And then we come up with a plan to help him accom-plish all those things. (Really, this isn't much different from what we already talked about with using volunteers.)

## 3. View the internship as a teaching opportunity.

Interns aren't people who do the work you don't like doing. In fact, having interns will probably cost you more time because you should make an effort to invest in each individual. Don't give an assignment and then turn your intern loose without teaching him how to do it well. Ensure that he's successful.

## 4. Always back your interns 100 percent.

Your interns need to know that you believe in them, that you sup-port them, and that you trust them. After you've equipped them, remain as hands-off as possible in their area of ministry. When they fail and make mistakes, see #3.

## 5. Prepare your interns for life, not just for ministry.

Ministry training is important, but developing your interns' spiri-tual lives, their character, their knowledge of Scripture, and their prayer life is even more important and will ultimately impact their ministry in profound ways.

## 6. Meet with each intern once a week.

Don't just give your interns a few youth group assignments and let them go. Meet regularly to review, debrief, follow up on assign-ments, pray together, study Scripture, encourage them and thank them for their investment in teenagers (even if it does cause you more work!).

## 7. Push your interns a little farther than they think they can go.

Don't let them stay in their comfort zone—make them take their ministry to the next level. We all need to be stretched from time to time, especially when we have someone else there to support us and cheer us on.

## 8. Find areas of weakness, but focus on strengths.

While it's necessary to address areas of weakness, don't focus on making those areas strong. Instead, focus on helping your intern use the strengths God's already given him. We all have weaknesses—that's okay. That's why we're a part of the body of Christ.

## 9. Let your intern tag along.

Some of the best teaching opportunities will come as your interns just hang out with you and shadow you in ministry. They'll start to ask questions, observe what you do, and might even provide insights into your routine that you never thought of before.

## 10. Invite them to critically evaluate the ministry.

Interns become more involved in the ministry than regular volunteers, so encourage them to always offer their perspectives for improvement and necessary changes. It's amazing the observations they'll make that you'll never see.

## 11. Keep your expectations high.

Hold interns accountable to their commitment and make sure they follow through in their areas of ministry. As you attempt to be as hands-off as possible, remind them that there's no backup plan if they drop the ball. If they don't follow through, address it frankly with the intern and remember that there's always room for mercy.

## 12. Make it age-appropriate.

If you have an intern who's a freshman or sophomore in college, assign them to the junior high. It's difficult for a young intern to earn respect as a leader with high school students who are close to his own age—especially if the intern graduated from your ministry and knows the upperclassmen. Plus, it may be tough for an intern to successfully exercise authority over his own peer group in situations that require discipline.

## Other Voices

**Mike Kupferer:**

Personally, I'm always leery of having an intern be someone who grew up in the youth group. I think that interns need to see a different way of doing ministry and learn how to get to know and work with people they don't already know.

**Justin Ross:**

I have the opportunity to hire an intern each summer. In my experiences, this list is fantastic. Just to expand on #4: Let interns know you have their back in every situation. If anyone has a problem with something they do, it goes though me. I take full responsibility for everything that happens. All complaints come to me—not the new guy. Any heat that comes from elders, parents, or volunteers goes though me. Then I talk with my intern about the problem and what we can do to fix it.

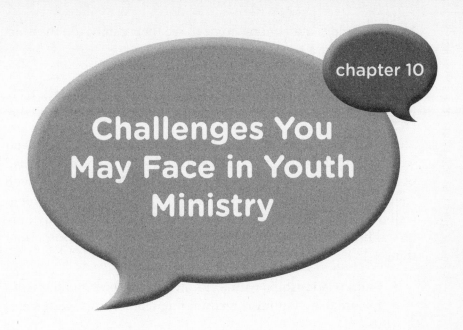

# chapter 10

# Challenges You May Face in Youth Ministry

## the hardest part of youth ministry

It's not all the meetings, reports, event planning, vision casting, or trainings. It's not even working with upset parents, disappointed church leaders, or the feeling of being unappreciated and misunderstood.

The hardest part of youth ministry is the emotional toll it takes to be involved with teens' lives and see them give in to the deceit of sin despite what they know to be right—it breaks my heart. But it reminds me how often I do the same. Now I understand a little of how God must feel about me.

## Other Voices

**Glenn W. Davies:**
For me, the hardest part of ministry is to see a teen come to Christ then decide to go back to the world, the influences of their old friends, and the bondage they were redeemed from. Sometimes I feel like a complete failure in ministry.

**Ebere Samuel:**
For me, one of my concerns is the idea that the change expected in young people has to be made possible by the youth worker. Most times the role of parents and other stakeholders isn't taken seriously. Imagine the confusion a teen faces hearing godly instruction

from the pulpit, but coming home to see their parents do the exact opposite. What a confusion.

## the daunting job description of a youth worker

More than any other ministry, youth ministry can be very overwhelming with everything that needs to be done and is expected of us. How in the world can it be possible to fulfill everything with some level of equal success? We know it's better to do a few things well than do many things halfway, but there really isn't anything on our list that can be cut out or eliminated—they're all important things!

- Build relationships with teens and spend time on their turf.
- Ensure that volunteers are building relationships with teens, too.
- Train and equip volunteers to be effective in their various roles.
- Train parents and provide resources for them to be godly spiritual leaders.
- Prepare ministry summary reports for church leadership.
- Prepare teens spiritually, emotionally, and mentally for life after high school.
- Plan, organize, and evaluate youth programs and then re-plan, reorganize, and re-evaluate them all over again.
- Work to earn a voice and respect in the church community.
- Become an expert on almost all teen issues, including—but not limited to—suicide, cutting, eating disorders, homosexuality, death, divorce, school dropouts, hazing, incest, depression, pregnancy, rape, smoking, peer pressure, STDs, drug and alcohol abuse, sexual abuse, emotional abuse, and verbal abuse.
- Become an effective communicator in both speech and writing.
- Stay up to date on youth culture, trends, and value systems.
- Develop counseling and listening skills.
- Cast a vision and recruit others to come on board.
- Keep a current and accurate budget.
- Learn to correctly handle God's Word.
- Maintain a healthy personal walk with God.

- Enjoy downtime so you can relax.
- Make sure God, spouse, and family are placed before everything else.

Youth pastors have to work with almost everyone: teens, parents, church leadership, and volunteers. How in the world is it possible to keep all these balls rolling at the same time, plus everything else I didn't even mention here, with only 40-50 hours per week? (Or even less if you're part time or a volunteer!)

If we're not careful, this is can be a perfect recipe for overload and burnout.

## Other Voices

### Tom Kay:

I'm not sure it's possible to be an expert in all the teen issues. It's critical for those of us on the front lines of student ministry to know when to ask for help or suggest help from professionals. That doesn't alleviate our responsibility to stay involved in a teen's life. We need to know when to refer and then continue to walk alongside those teens struggling with the issues you mentioned. Any way you slice it, it's a tough gig. Worth every minute, but tough.

### Jerry Schmoyer:

You forgot—educate the rest of the church who often think a youth pastor is nothing more than a recreation director on a cruise ship who plays games and gets paid for acting like a teen.

### Mike Morris:

I like the image of keeping all the balls in the air. Although for youth ministry I would add that another person is always throwing more balls at you while you're trying to juggle.

# mistakes that can kill your ministry's growth

If you're not careful, there are several key mistakes that'll hinder your youth ministry's growth and direction.

## Thinking you know everything.

Typically, youth workers are a bit younger, and unfortunately we often fit the stereotype of being a little too overconfident— sometimes even arrogant. We all need to make sure we're open to suggestions, advice, and input from others and that our life-long journey of learning is never done. Most of us probably like to think we're open to correction, but sometimes that means we're only open to it if we're clearly proven to be in the wrong.

While other areas of your church's ministry may remain pretty consistent from year to year, youth ministry is unique in that the people you're working with change every year. Each year you'll meet new incoming students and say farewell to the graduating seniors. Just because you think you've got this ministry thing down this year doesn't mean it won't need to be changed next year, because each year you'll be working with a different group of teens. Be open to learning and hearing from teens, parents, church staff, and other leaders.

## Getting wrapped up in marketing hype.

There are so many different youth ministry products, services, curricula, and people who say you need to buy such-and-such to make your ministry successful that it's hard not to get sucked in. It may even feel like you can't do ministry without a big budget. There are a lot of good sales pitches out there where you'll buy something that's worth close to nothing, and there's a lot of unknown material that's absolutely worth every penny you spend on it. If you're considering a purchase, start by talking to some people you trust and get their input. Also try to find someone who's actually used the product and listen to what he has to say about it. Search for a review on a blog somewhere, on Amazon.com's reviews, or ask for opinions on MinistryQuestions.com to get an objective opinion. Just don't get sucked into hype over products that may or may not be what your group really needs.

## Not taking action.

If you read a book or hear something that's particularly challenging to you and your ministry and you know that what the book proposes would make a positive impact on your ministry, actually do it. Reading and listening to wiser people without acting on their advice and wisdom won't do you or your ministry a bit of good.

## Worrying about what others think.

There will always be people who criticize you and your ministry. Always. Their opinions are valuable if they're on your side, if they've also been encouraging and supportive in the past, and if they've demonstrated that they truly have the best interest of the ministry at heart. But if you're sucked into always worrying about what other people are going to think about you, what they're going to say, or who they'll talk to behind your back, then maybe you have some real security issues you need to work through. That doesn't mean you should disregard good, honest, godly advice—but if you're always scared of what others will say, or you're in ministry because deep down you need people to approve of you and what you do, that's going to be a hindrance. You need to find your validation from the Lord, not others around you. If you're a leader, it doesn't matter what you do or where you serve, you will be criticized.

## Dabbling with it.

Sometimes we dabble with lots of ideas and goals without whole-heartedly committing to anything. Too often we start a program, begin a regular prayer meeting, or start running with an idea, but then get distracted when the next shiny idea catches our attention. If you start something, pour yourself into it. If later you decide it's not working and you need to change or end it, that's fine—just don't keep jumping around. If you jump around too much, your ministry will seem as though it has no direction, and the momentum you're trying to build will be killed.

## Maintaining unrealistic expectations.

Maybe you read a book that says, "If you do A, B, and C, then your ministry will explode and be wildly successful!" So you tried A, B, and C, but nothing happened. Nothing changed. Or maybe your ministry even struggled harder. Have realistic expectations for your ministry, for yourself, for your leaders, for your church, and for your teenagers. Yes, it's disappointing to plan an event and have no one show up—it can be even more disappointing when you feel more people should be coming to Christ through your ministry. That's why it's helpful to set realistic expectations and know that God's in control. Ultimately, the Holy Spirit is responsible for the life-change you desperately want to see.

## Not taking responsibility for you.

If you're in youth ministry, you probably have a heart that loves teens and wants to do everything possible to serve them. While that's noble, you first need to take care of yourself. If you don't take care of your own health and energy level, then you'll be of little or no use to anyone else. Exercise often, sleep well, and take advantage of all of your vacation days so the Lord can use you to your maximum potential throughout your entire life.

## Not investing in your spiritual life.

Make sure you're spending time with the Lord. The best resource any youth group can have is a youth leader who's growing and digging into God's Word on a personal level—someone who's becoming more and more passionate about God every day. That passion tends to become contagious and rub off on the teens around you.

## Other Voices

### Kyle Galle:

The one that struck a chord with me is taking care of myself. In the town where I work, there are many youth pastors who don't take care of themselves. They work too many hours, don't take time off, are afraid to let someone else handle something—and they're starting to burn out. I try to tell them they need to take time for themselves, but it doesn't work (I'm the newbie in town). This is the Achilles' heel of youth pastors.

### Justin Ross:

Good list here. It's also important to point out that football season can kill your ministry's growth.

At different times of the school year, it's very possible your ministry will not grow much. A few years back, our local high school football team won the state championship. It was the first time this community made it past the first couple of rounds of the playoffs. For the month leading up to that championship game, our youth ministry took a nosedive. The football players, cheerleaders, band members, ROTC, and all the teens in video production were slammed. All of the other teenagers were more excited about school than they ever had been. And few of them were making it to youth group.

If your ministry isn't growing, look over this list. If you're not making any of these mistakes, take a look at what's going on at school and in the community. Then don't take it personally—send tons of encouraging text messages, and soon things will get back to normal.

### Aaron Giesler:

Lack of communication with the church leadership can not only kill growth, but can also cost you your job. You boss (whether it be a senior pastor or some other person) doesn't like surprises, especially when they're bad ones. Communicating good news and even bad news can go a long way to bolster trust with your boss and make things run smoothly. Your supervisor can also help you avoid mistakes. If you're thinking about trying an outreach event that failed two years ago under another youth worker, he can talk to you about that event.

# dealing with the pressures of church leadership

Pressures of church leadership—we all experience it. How we handle it, however, probably varies from person to person. Here's what works for me:

### Spend time in the Word and in prayer.

I don't see how people can make it in ministry by only depending on their own strength, their own "wisdom," and their own vision. Christ must be our focus.

### Earn the trust and respect of the congregation.

If you've invested in earning the congregation's trust in little things, when the big issues arise you're more likely to have their support.

### Develop relationships with church leadership.

Know the team in which God has placed you and learn to work together in all areas of ministry—not just in your individual areas of responsibility. When pressure comes, it's a lot easier when their support and understanding are already in place.

### Learn to say no.

As I've said many times, setting boundaries is vital not only for maintaining a healthy personal life, but for maintaining a positive view of ministry. It's easy to feel overwhelmed, because there's always more you feel you could be doing.

### Maintain an accurate perspective of ministry.

God doesn't need you to take care of his ministry—he only chooses to use you as a vessel. So don't feel like the ministry belongs to you or depends on you. The people ultimately belong to God, and he can take care of them with or without your involvement.

### Know your vision and communicate it clearly and often.

People naturally rally behind those who have a vision and who are developing a strategy to accomplish it. Don't get so focused on the little details that you lose sight of the big picture. If you do, those following you will, too, and suddenly no one will know where they're going.

## Spend time doing your favorite hobby.

Whether that be playing video games, reading, sitting by a lake, or playing with your children, recreation and rest are essential for you to be the leader God desires you to be.

## Other Voices

**Mike Kupferer:**

Knowing (and believing) that the elders/church leadership are behind you and will support you relieves a lot of pressure to try to make everyone happy. And even though we say we know it's impossible to make everyone happy, I think we still (at times) want to. When you know you have the support of others in leadership, then you can be more confident in your actions. This comes from spending time with your church leadership and getting to know them. Let them see you and your heart so they'll know your desire for growth and can stand up for you when negative comments are thrown your way.

# handing discipline as a young youth worker

A 25-year-old who had worked in three different churches told me that his biggest challenge is handling discipline. As a young man, his authority was not always respected by the teens because—in some ways—he still looked like a teenager.

When he asked for advice, several ideas came to my mind from my time when I was a 19-year-old youth pastor. Here's what I told him:

## Establish yourself as the leader from the very beginning.

Although you are close to their age, you're their leader before you're their friend. Just having the title of youth pastor and the backing of the church leadership sets you apart, so don't be afraid to use your authority.

## Don't be afraid to discipline.

Studies have shown that parents who discipline are shown more respect and love from their teens, because discipline proves to the teens that their parents love them. It makes teens feel like someone cares enough to correct them and give them some direction in life. In youth ministry you're the leader of the group, so you set the tone and standards for what happens. Then enforce your decisions.

## Be consistent.

If you say there are certain consequences for an offense, follow through with those consequences. Although it will be hard the first few times, you'll earn their respect and they'll learn to trust your word when you say something.

## Don't be timid because you're young.

Be assertive, take charge, and do whatever is necessary to manage the group. Again, you're the leader. If they don't respect your authority, the group may become chaotic and ministry effectiveness will dwindle.

Basically, it comes down to being tough and establishing yourself as the person in charge. Hopefully you can do this by earning the teenagers' trust and respect. If not, you may have to enforce it in other ways whether they like it or not. It's part of your job.

Officially setting some boundaries on paper is a good idea, too. Just make sure everything you state is enforceable and that you appropriately follow up when violations occur—otherwise your boundaries will lose credibility and be pointless. If you write something, make sure you state everything in a positive way, emphasizing each point's benefit to the ministry and those involved. You don't want a big list of dos and don'ts that will feel restrictive. Instead, you want to establish guidelines that will empower the teens.

Remember that discipline should be done within the context of building a relationship. Whenever I have to talk to a teenager for acting inappropriately or disrespectfully, I always do my best to do two things:

1. Address the situation, not the teenager personally. Don't attack his character as if he were causing trouble just to make youth group difficult for you. Let him know that you're not angry with him, but that whatever action he just displayed was inappropriate.
2. Affirm the teenager afterward. Let him know you still love him. Give him positive attention, express your excitement when he shows up at youth group, say goodbye to him as he leaves, and so on.

## Other Voices

### Gregg Jacobs:

One thing that helped me is to establish consequences for breaking the rules. We called it the Three Strike Rule. First, you warn the teen and let him know what will happen if he continues to disrupt the group. Second, you move him so he won't be tempted to disrupt. Third, you remove him and talk to his parents. I rarely get to the third strike with most church teenagers. With teens who don't have family in the church, this can be hard to deal with. I've seen it happen where those unchurched parents just say that their teenager won't be back. That stinks. But I'd rather have a group of teens who can participate, learn, and experience God than a group that has free run of the place. Don't worry about teens not coming because of rules. If you have a place where they can experience life and the real Jesus, they'll come.

### Jenna Gilbertson:

I think the biggest thing—especially for a young youth worker—is follow-through. I had some boys on a retreat who were behaving really badly. They were disrespecting me and the other leaders. After two warnings, we sat them down, spoke very seriously with them, and had them turn the contents of their pockets out. I took away the items that were causing distractions and told them I was going to call their parents when I got home. They begged me not to, but I did call their parents. I explained to the parents that I was their teens' youth director, and I wanted the teens to be able to trust me and to know that what I'm saying is true—both the good and the bad. They and the other teens who heard about it take me seriously now. And yet, they know I still love them. Follow-through . . . big deal!

### Chris Goeppner:

Most of the teens I deal with have never been disciplined outside of a classroom. In these situations I ask the Lord for wisdom and words.

### Aaron Giesler:

I also experienced this when I was a 19-year-old youth pastor. The leaders in the church perpetuated it, because they set the driving age to 20. One of the parents also told her teen that he didn't have to mind me because he had a brother older than I was. I had to address it with the leadership and how they had hired me and then set me up to fail. Then, I had to address the issue with the parent and the senior pastor. After that, things went better. Not great, but better.

## the difficult and disruptive teen

We've all had them: teens who cause trouble, play on their cell phones while you teach, are disrespectful, and generally appear mad at the world. Although we love these teenagers as much as we love the cooperative ones, sometimes it feels as though we're sacrificing the quality of the ministry to all the other teens for the sake of that one (or three, or whatever) disruptive teen.

When I had my first encounter with this kind of situation, my senior pastor at the time gave me some advice and I've followed it ever since: Never sacrifice the ministry to all the teens for the sake of one, or even a couple. If—because of one or a few disruptive teenagers—other teens in the group aren't receiving the attention they need, the spiritual input they seek, and time to focus on God, then a course of action is needed.

Of course, every situation is unique, so this should be tailored accordingly, but here's a framework to help you get started:

### 1. Talk with the teenager privately.
Ask why she comes to youth group, and share that her actions make you feel as if she doesn't want to be there. Affirm her as a person, but confront her actions. Give her a chance to change her attitude on her own.

### 2. If it continues, talk with the teen again.
This time, tell her that if things don't change by next week, you're going to talk with her parents about it (if applicable). If nothing changes, follow through by calling or meeting with her parents.

### 3. If the issues continue after that, talk with your senior pastor about the situation.
As your supervisor, he needs to be in the loop about the course of action you decide on together. If the plan doesn't go smoothly, you need to know ahead of time that your pastor supports the direction you take in handling this matter.

In case you need help coming up with a course of action, here's a plan that I sometimes use: First, speak privately with the teen again and tell her that she has one more week to change her behavior. If things aren't dramatically different at youth group next week, she'll be on a four-week probation from youth group. At the end of four weeks, she'll be welcome to return and try again. However, during that four weeks don't just send her away. Always discipline with the idea of restoration in mind—just as Christ does for us. Either you or another adult must meet with that teen one-on-one every week outside of church. Go out for lunch and talk about life and spiritual matters. Just because that teenager isn't permitted at youth group for four weeks doesn't mean she shouldn't receive spiritual encouragement from you and your ministry.

## 4. If the behavior continues, put the teen on probation again.

If you've met with the teenager one-on-one every week for four weeks and really loved on her, the chances are pretty high that her attitude problem will be gone when she returns, because she'll have a new respect and trust for you, the leader. But—in the rare situation that her disruptive behavior continues—you must put her on probation again. This time she'll be on probation for three months, six months, or whatever you and your pastor deem appropriate. But only do so knowing that you or someone else on your team is going to meet with that teenager one-on-one every week during that time.

A variation of this is to start meeting one-on-one with the teen outside of church even before you get to step number three (which I'd probably advise anyway if at all possible). The difference is that the one-on-one meetings are still optional, whereas in step #3, the individual meeting time is required if the teen is going to be permitted back at youth group again.

## Other Voices

**Rob Finkill:**
Regarding the cell phone issue, we've been using one of those hanging shoe caddies as a place to store phones. Our teens leave them there as they check in for service. Each space is labeled with a name of a teen for their phone and/or iPod. It's worked well. We laid the foundation for it a few weeks ahead of time and explained to teens and parents the reasons for it.

**Justin Ross:**
I heard a phrase several years ago that I've since used over and over. When you need to contact the parents, instead of telling them there's a problem, say, "I need your help with something."

It won't put parents on the defensive and it doesn't communicate that you're angry at their teen—even though you may be! I've always had a positive response when I began tough conversations this way.

## dealing with drama at youth group

Anyone who works with teenagers quickly becomes familiar with drama. Gossip spreads and the whole, "You're not my friend this week because you sat with so-and-so at school instead of me" thing takes place.

Here are some tips that might be helpful in this situation:

### Saturate the ministry in prayer.

By this point in the book I know I probably sound like a broken record in regard to the importance of prayer, but it's too often a key point youth workers miss! Sure, we pray to open and close meetings—but what about spending hours soaking the ministry in prayer? This should be happening anyway, but if it isn't, now's a good time to start. Service to the Lord always starts with prayer. The difference between a ministry saturated in prayer and one that isn't is amazing! I think we often underestimate prayer and think our time is better spent doing ministry.

### Pick your battles.

Some drama is worth our intervention and some isn't. If we get involved in every small event, we'll soon become very frustrated and lose our credibility for when the big issues arise. Be willing to let the minor issues slide. Teens are capable of solving some problems on their own.

### Be intentional about building relationships with the "drama queens."

I've noticed that drama usually starts with a few key people and spreads from there. Make sure that you or another adult leader are taking time to invest in each of the "extra care required" teens on an ongoing basis. Earn the trust and respect of these teens so that when you need to address the drama, there's a relationship context already in place. Teens will be more apt to listen to someone who's proven that they care than they will to someone who's just a youth group authority figure.

### Address the drama in love.

No matter how frustrated you may feel, be careful about standing in front of a group and condemning them all. Instead, sit down with each teen and within the context of the relationship you've already built, speak with her about it. "Hey Sarah, Jennifer looks pretty upset that she's not your friend this week just because she sat with Holly at school last week. Why's it so important to you that she always sit with you?"

### Use each drama issue as a teaching moment.

We all know that the best teaching moments are not the times we stand in front of a group and preach a mini-sermon. The best teaching moments are the everyday real-life situations that we're privileged to be a part of. This includes the drama. If appropriate and both parties are willing, bring them together to apologize. Use passages like Ephesians 4:29 and Romans 12:18—not in a preachy way, but as a reminder that this is how Scripture applies to our life.

### Be willing to go through the process many times.

Drama issues are not a once-in-a-lifetime experience. They'll be ongoing—usually within the same groups of teenagers. Be patient with these teens. God's more than patient with us in all our short-comings. Be willing to sit down and address the major drama issues in love as often as necessary. Challenge the teens to grow rather than expecting them to come to youth group as perfectly mature people.

### Make sure that youth group remains a safe place.

In extreme cases when inappropriate situations arise that can be physically or emotionally harmful to other individuals, discipline is necessary. As much as it pains us to do so, a student may need to be dismissed from youth group for a time. Never sacrifice the whole group for the sake of keeping one or two students around. If certain teenagers are involved with the dismissed teen, you may need to talk with them privately, and explain what's going on. But don't tell the whole youth group and make a spectacle out of the teen. Follow Christ's example and always discipline with the idea of restoration in mind. Communicate love throughout the whole process.

### Have realistic expectations.

Remember that teenagers are still growing and maturing. Don't expect youth group to be a place devoid of drama or conflict.

Instead, love your teenagers, guide them through the restoration process when necessary, use their experiences as teaching experiences, and encourage them to resolve some conflict on their own.

## Other Voices

### Chris Day:

We have 80-90 middle school students every week—this creates so much drama it's not even funny. For the most part, a lot of it goes away as teens mature. But some teens can't escape drama. It's like they're drama magnets. These are the ones I call the "high-maintenance" teens. I love them, but they can really suck the life out of you if you're not careful.

My advice is to help them find a leader they can relate to. Separate the dramatic teens as much as possible. Take outings with the teens who cause the drama. Help them establish a bond of friendship with each other—sometimes that helps the drama go away as well. If these teens find they have a common bond, that may help them learn to trust and value each other.

### Steve Blanchard:

I've experienced drama with my staff. I'm the new guy and the staff has been involved in the youth ministry for a long time. They'd complain to the elders and then the elders would come to me. This is unhealthy, by the way. The best thing to do is address problems immediately before others feel the wave of someone complaining. If it's with love, you can do this with any of the people that help you. Usually it's always a few influential people who stir the pot, so go to the people with influence and make sure you're clear with them.

# ministry: grind or glamour?

Sometimes I forget that ministry is more grind than glamour Looking at youth ministry from the outside, it can be easy to think that it's just about playing games, hanging out with teens, and going on cool retreats—a grand ol' time for everyone.

Although these elements are fun, I'm learning more and more over the years that real ministry is not as glamorous as it seems. Real ministry is messy. It's about getting into sticky areas of depraved lives and doing whatever's necessary to encourage growth and maturity. When it requires confrontation, it's very difficult, awkward, and stressful. This is not glamorous at all.

## Other Voices

**Zac Wheeler:**

That's the awful truth. But I couldn't picture myself anywhere else.

**Tom Cottar:**

Dude, community is messy! Especially when confrontation is involved, like you mention. It's painful a lot of times, but I believe the fruit will be worth the pruning. I wouldn't trade student ministry for any "greener pastures."

**Justin Ross:**

Youth ministry is such a honor. Those of us who have been called to it get to wake up each day and live our dream. Sure, it's a grind and oftentimes not very glamorous, but many people in the world would give anything to be able to get paid for their passion. We're that lucky. And to me, that's amazing.

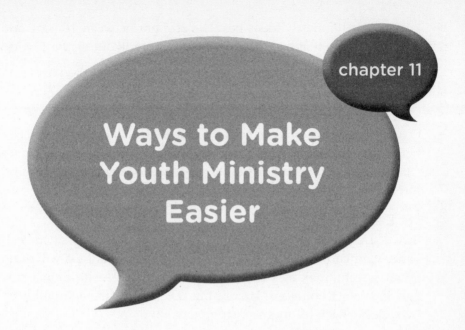

# chapter 11

# Ways to Make Youth Ministry Easier

## 11 ways to reduce stress in ministry

It's not uncommon for a youth worker to feel maxed out, tired, and drained. Unlike some other vocations, youth ministry is not just physically and mentally exhausting—it's also emotionally draining, which only enhances the stress.

Here are eleven ways (in reverse order) to reduce stress in ministry.

### 11. Take regular breaks.

Ministry workers are usually workaholics. There are appropriate times when you need to buckle down and crunch through some work, but when it's done, leave your workplace for a few minutes. Go outside, walk around, and get some sun. You'll be amazed how refreshed you feel coming back. A 10–15 minute break outside can really energize you to finish the rest of your work in much better time and with higher quality, too.

### 10. Work when you focus best.

It seems like most people I know in ministry are early-morning people. They love waking up before the sun and hitting the office early. If that's what works best for you, then do it! However, some people—like me—think that mornings are a result of the fall in Genesis 3 and can't function until lunchtime. I work well all afternoon, but I honestly focus best late at night between 10 p.m. and 2 a.m. During that time is when I tend to crank out my best work. Find out what works best for you and capitalize on it.

## 9. Address the work at home.

Stacks of bills, car maintenance, yard work, and home repairs can really stress you out—especially if it seems like everything else going on in life is always a higher priority. If tasks start piling up at home, take an extra day off to get it all done and set your mind free.

## 8. Eat healthy foods.

Give your body the food that will keep you well nourished. Balance your carbs, fruits, vegetables, and grains. Junk food will drain your system, making you tired and unfocused. A sugar rush may give you small bursts of energy, but the crash at the end will keep you going back for more sugar all day long.

## 7. Stay in shape.

It's clinically proven that regular exercise reduces stress, gives you more energy, improves your sleep at night, and helps you stay more alert during the day. There's really no excuse not to stay in shape, especially for people in ministry. And if you have tight muscles and achy joints, see a massage therapist or a chiropractor.

## 6. Use your vacation days.

Many of us are happy with our jobs, our ministries, and the work we do, but there are always small things about each job that we hate. That's just a part of life. Over time, those annoyances can build until they overshadow what we really do enjoy. Make sure you take a break—time to rest, time to get away, and time to leave it all behind. If your ministry can't function without you for a couple of days, the ministry is way too focused on you and is unhealthy.

## 5. Keep ministry simple.

Lots of activity and responsibilities may make you feel more important than you really are, but it's a guaranteed formula for stress and burnout. Know your limits and be realistic. If you have too much on your plate, delegate some of it to others—or simply cut it out of your life. If no one steps up to take over something in my ministry that I don't have time to do, it simply doesn't get done. It's really that easy.

## 4. Listen to worship music.

I don't mean just have it playing in the background—although that might help. Sit down and really listen to it. Let the Holy Spirit work in your life as you spend personal time in worship—thinking, reflecting, and meditating on him. All the stressful things in your life pale in comparison to a healthy reminder of who God is.

## 3. Say no!

I've said this before, but I don't know why ministry workers feel as if they must say yes to so many things. Maintain boundaries in your life. I'm a youth pastor and I only go to about half of our weekly youth meetings. I work hard to recruit and train solid volunteers so that the ministry works whether I'm there or not. If the ministry is centered on you, you're doing something wrong. You shouldn't be out more than three nights a week maximum. Be at home with your family.

## 2. Maintain healthy relationships with your spouse.

Remember, your primary ministry is to your family—especially your spouse. Don't wait until the relationship starts feeling dry to do something about it. Maintain the relationship so you never get to that point in the first place. Spend time alone together, go on dates, read the Word together, plan random romantic acts, be sexually active.

## 1. Focus on the Lord.

Regular time with the Lord is critical, but it often seems as if it's the first thing we set aside. Spend time with God on a personal level and also make him a priority for your family. You can't serve the Lord and follow him without knowing where he's leading you. Otherwise, you fall into a stale rut of just doing ministry, rather than leading a movement of God's people.

## Other Voices

**Jason Huffman:**
One thing I do to manage stress is I leave my work at the office. I know some people work well at home, but for me there are too many distractions and too much temptation to work instead of spend time with family. I don't check my office email unless I'm at the office. Likewise, I don't have a Blackberry or PDA set up to receive work-related emails at home. This allows me to focus on home stuff at home and office stuff at the office.

**Sara Evanchick:**

Well, I'm usually a ball of stress, but I've started something new that seems to be helping. I sit down at the beginning of the week and look at the tasks I need to get done and then I block out the time when I'm going to work on them. Instead of having a huge list of things that need to be done in the office during the week, I have a bite-sized list of things I'm going to do Monday morning, Monday afternoon, etc., I schedule tasks as I would meetings. This might not work for everyone, but it's changing my perspective and helping me feel less overwhelmed by the weeklong to-do list that puts me into a cold sweat.

**D.J. Butcher:**

I had to disconnect my church email from my home because I was constantly checking it. Of course when I would get something, I would go back into work mode and deal with whatever the email was about. I had enough and deleted the account at home. You know what happened? Those emails were still in my inbox at the church when I got back the next day and the world hadn't ended. Imagine that.

**Josh Christian:**

#5 seems to be the hardest across all forms of ministry. Not sure if it's the ego or outside pressure. This is one that I've gotten flack for quite a bit in ministry. It stinks that many times parents, volunteers, staff and even the teens expect you to do more than you can. That really makes it tough.

# living with a spouse who serves in youth ministry

The first half of this section comes from the perspective of my wife, Dana Schmoyer. She's been a faithful companion for me through many years of ministry and is incredible at balancing the roles of being a supporter, encourager, co-laborer, wife, and the voice of reason in my life.

Based on her experience with me, she has nine ideas for ministry wives about how to support and join their husbands in ministry. If you're a married guy in youth ministry, this may be a good section to pass along to your wife. If you're a married woman in youth ministry, skip past Dana's advice—there's a section you might want to share with your husband.

We all need the love and support of our spouse, so talk through some of these issues together. Since every marriage and ministry context is unique, discuss some other ideas you'd add to this list.

## For the woman whose husband is a youth worker:

### Have fun and be carefree.

Enjoy every moment you can. Don't let the little stuff stress you out. It's okay if your husband didn't plan the event the way you would've planned it or the teenagers accidentally break something at your house during Bible study.

A great way Tim has helped me to be carefree is by not telling me things that would probably upset me—such as someone either criticizing him or the youth ministry. When I hear those criticisms, I take them personally, and then I can't look at that person the same any more.

### Try something new.

I've found that teenagers really enjoy it when I'm willing to try something I haven't done—especially when I do it with them. I'm terrified of heights, and on our first canoe trip with our youth group we got to a part of the river with a bridge they always stop at to jump off. The teens were so excited for me to get up there and jump. When you try something new, it provides a great bonding time, and then you have stories to share with them. Also, a great way I have found to bond with the boys is to play video games or participate in sports with them. Ask God to show you a new way to build relationships with the youth, and be willing to stretch.

### Learn to say no.

Your husband needs to learn this, too. I learned that if you don't say yes a few times when invited to something, then you prob-ably won't be invited again, but when you say yes to everything, it becomes overwhelming. You can't make it to everything, and that's okay. It's good for teens to see you at their events, and it's a good time to get to know their families. It's also good that they see you model healthy boundaries. Go to teenagers' band concerts and plays with your spouse—but don't go to every one. People will understand if you don't make it to all the teens' extracurricular events.

### Surround yourself with other godly women.

It's good to have fellowship with other women—especially since many of us like to chat, and sometimes our husbands can't handle all that we want or need to talk about. Plus, after living with a man, it's nice to be around other females who can relate to all of our womanly quirks. Make sure the women are godly so that you can lift each other up in prayer, encouragement, and accountability.

**Be present.**

It's easy for a teen girl to develop a crush on her youth pastor—especially if he's hot (like my husband!). I've seen a few girls crush on Tim, which is tough. My feelings toward them change and I find it hard to be as friendly. The spiritual aspect of any relationship becomes intimate—that's why we're to surround ourselves with other godly women, not men. Wives, if the students see you regularly (I know this is probably harder if you have kids), and your public interaction with your husband shows that you two are totally in love, girls will know he's romantically interested in you, not them. Husbands, if you aren't quick to catch on, then ask your wife to help you notice signs of a crush. Be aware of how often girls call or text you, and be cautious about how frequently you respond. If you respond every time, they'll likely contact you even more frequently. Guys should also be aware that another sign of flirting is when a girl takes a boy's hat. (I'm pretty sure any girl who has gone through junior high knows this.) Tim doesn't make a big deal of it when girls do it to him—he ignores the action, and it soon stops.

Wives, let your husband minister to the boys, and you get to know the girls in order to be a positive spiritual role model for them. This can help a girl feel comfortable around you, so that when she wants to talk with your husband, you can be present. Tim and I love to take a girl out to eat when she needs closer attention. If you've already been present in her life, it's not weird for you to be there as a chaperone.

**Set boundaries.**

Make sure the two of you are clear on how many nights a week your husband is going to be out. (Tim and I try to keep it to three nights a week.) Some weeks we've had something every night, but then we make sure the following week is close to empty. Also, protect your home. I have known people to open their house to teens, letting them drop in at any time of the day or night. I highly recommend against this. Your house should be a sanctuary. By protecting your home you're protecting time with your family.

**Speak carefully.**

I mentioned earlier that it's important to surround yourself with godly women. If you're involved with women from church with whom you feel you can share everything, that's great, but watch what you say. You can be open with these friends without sharing intimate details of your marriage or personal issues in ministry. Find a godly woman outside of your church circle with whom you can share personal details about your life and ministry.

If you're not married but are dating a youth pastor, don't share details of your relationship with others in the church. I made that mistake and speak from experience—it quickly turned into gossip.

## Always support your husband publicly.

No matter what, support him in public. If you disagree with something, tell your husband when no one's around. If someone comes to you with a complaint, you can listen, but don't try to fix the problem. That person needs to go directly to him. God put you here to support your husband—not to carry him.

## Be sexually active with your husband.

Sex is a good stress reliever and fulfills his needs, which helps prevent temptations for him. Likewise, husbands, make sure you are meeting your wife's emotional needs.

Neither Dana nor I felt qualified to give advice to the husbands of female youth workers, so these following suggestions are from a friend of mine named Patti Gibbons. She's served in youth ministry for more than 20 years, all of them (plus a few more) married to her husband Tom, who has been in the military and law enforcement during those years. Patti will be the first to tell you that they're still figuring this "life in student ministry" stuff out, but obviously they haven't made it through 20 years without learning a few things along the way.

## For the guy whose wife is a youth pastor:

### Take good care of your marriage.

It's been particularly important for me, as the one in ministry and leadership, to ensure that my husband is affirmed in his role as the spiritual leader of our household. His spiritual role in our family is unaltered by mine in ministry with teens and families. (This is in addition to all of the marriage and relationship pointers Dana mentions above.)

### Be accountable to each other.

Because the churches and ministries where I've served have brought me alongside more male coworkers than female coworkers, it's important that my husband and I maintain a high level of accountability with one another. Keeping each other in the loop about where and when we're meeting or working with someone of the opposite gender has kept the opportunity for gossip, hurt feelings, or bitterness out of play.

### Be discerning.
Because of the different ways men and women often approach problem solving, when an issue of criticism about me or the ministry would arise, it was difficult for my husband to hold back from jumping to my defense. Openly support your wife, but it's also important to be discerning about when—or if—you should publicly defend your ministry wife over an issue in which you're not directly involved.

### Travel together whenever possible.
On those occasions when your wife needs to travel for trips or camps, try to go along to support and encourage her—see her work in her element. Knowing that you're there just for her is a huge way you can serve her.

### You're not the complaint department.
This may seem too simple, but it's important for my husband to know that he's not the suggestion box or the complaint department for the youth ministry. He's gotten practice over the years at saying, "I'm sure Patti would listen to what you're telling me—give her a call."

### Find your own place to grow and serve.
Take the opportunity to get involved with the ministry if—and only if—you're called to do so. If you're not inclined or gifted for youth ministry, it's all right! Find a ministry that fits your gifts and talents, and get plugged in. Your spiritual health and growth is the greatest gift you can give your ministry spouse. Having a male friend—or group of friends—with whom you study and have accountability is important to your growth and keeps you strong so that your leadership of your ministry wife and your family won't suffer.

## Other Voices

### Adam Walker Cleaveland:
I think Dana's advice might work for some couples. However, my wife is currently working toward getting a PhD, and so many of these suggestions just don't work for our situation. She works extremely hard—and puts in long hours for her school. She's supportive of me and helps me think of youth group games, program ideas, and lots

of other stuff. She's also a very helpful person for me when I need someone to talk through certain issues that come up in the ministry. But as for her going to lots of events with me, being around the ministry a lot, being able to say yes to almost anything—it just doesn't work for our situation. Because of my wife's busy schedule, she just doesn't have the time to say yes to almost anything.

**Cindy Coker:**
As the mother of two young boys (two years old and four years old), I've had to realize that I can't do everything the way I did before we had children. I have to take care of my boys' needs first. Many activities cut into their naptime and bedtime. That means I have to stay home while my husband is attending an activity. I miss a lot of fun stuff for now—but I know this is just a season in our life. Soon the children will be old enough to go with us. We're very thankful for willing female youth sponsors who fill in the gap for me. It's been a humbling experience for me—a person who wants to do it all. I've had to step back and examine where I need to be to stay obedient to God's will. Sometimes that means I'm with the youth group and sometimes I need to stay home with our children.

**Luke Trouten:**
When I started in youth ministry I found that it was very easy to choose youth group over marriage. It's not hard to justify "God's work" as more important than date night. The thing is, over your life you'll minister to hundreds of teens, each of whom has potentially dozens of people pouring into their lives. But you have only one spouse, and that's it.

**Eric Helton:**
I've made the mistake of telling my wife about problems at the church or about people who have attacked me or the youth program. This does put a strain on my ministry and the people God has entrusted me to minister to. We should be considerate and loving enough toward our spouse that we would do anything to keep her worship intact. My wife loves God, but at times I've noticed that she doesn't feel comfortable going to church to worship and that's usually after I've put my mouth in drive before cranking my brain. Be considerate and keep church problems at church.

**Ryan Peduzzi:**
I believe that Dana's last point about being sexually active is extremely important for both the youth pastor as well as the spouse—and I'm not just saying that because I'm a guy. I feel the

heart of this point is to remember to give to your spouse, and work to meet his needs. As a minister you have to give so much to so many people, that it's easy to come home and just shut down. You need to remember the importance of the marital relationship and that you need to give to and meet the needs of your spouse, whether that's the man's sexual needs, or the women's emotional needs. So, don't come home at the end of the day with nothing left. Instead remember to save some of your time, energy, and care to give to your spouse, and make the intentional effort to do so. This type of giving will not just happen on its own—you must make the effort to prepare, plan, and give.

**Ruth Elkin:**

As a woman in youth ministry there are times when I need someone who's removed from my work situation to talk about some of the more painful or emotional struggles. As a married couple we've discovered that when we discuss some of these situations I've experienced, I'm left feeling better for having shared, but my husband is frustrated for me about the situation. It's been a process for us both to learn how much is appropriate for me to share so that my husband is not frustrated, and we can still feel close in our marriage.

## advantages of a local network of youth workers

Every Tuesday at 9 a.m. I meet with a few other youth pastors from different churches in my community. The churches that are actively involved in our youth worker network hold very similar theological beliefs. All of us are extremely comfortable sending students to each other's ministries, partnering for events and meetings, and even teaching each other's youth groups.

There's a lot more to like about the group: the fun, the teasing, the transparency, the support, and the benefit of a neutral party off of whom to bounce ideas and struggles—but the thing I value most is that we share a kingdom-mindset approach to ministry. In fact, there was a point about a year ago when we tossed around the idea of eliminating each of our individual church's youth ministries and linking arms to create a single, community-wide youth ministry with each of us who are paid by our different churches in the area serving as full-time staff together.

Here's how the kingdom mindset works in our youth ministries:

- Instead of each church doing individual training, we pool resources and fly someone in once a year to do an all-day training for all of our youth leaders combined.
- Sometimes I send teens from my youth group to the other churches for their events. They sometimes do the same for our events. If someone else's ministry is doing something solid, why not join it?
- We have friendly competition between youth groups—such as our multi-youth group dodgeball tournament.
- We support each other's ministries by spreading the word about each other's events and meetings. For example, in January 2010 the other churches sent all their parents to my church for a Real World Parents seminar and helped with childcare for the event.
- We hear each other's struggles, offer support and encouragement, and pray for each other. It's great to have a neutral place to talk about our challenges.
- We learn together by reading and discussing various books, such as *Youth Ministry 3.0: A Manifesto of Where We've Been, Where We Are, and Where We Need to Go* by Mark Oestreicher and *Seven Practices of Effective Ministry* by Andy Stanley, Lane Jones, and Reggie Joiner.
- We used to have combined monthly youth meetings, but after a couple years it started to dwindle and the vision for it faded, so we canned it in 2008. The value of bringing all our groups together for worship, teaching, and connection with each other was definitely positive, though, because it reinforced a kingdom-mindset value for the teenagers in our groups.
- We share resources with each other. One church has a bus that we've all borrowed; another church lets us use their way-cool sanctuary for senior high small group baptisms; we even share extra food with each other's ministries so it doesn't go to waste.
- Some of the youth groups have been known to cancel their youth meeting and go crash someone else's youth group meeting instead.
- There's open communication about problem teens and families who flip-flop churches.

- Each of the youth pastors occasionally serves as a guest teacher in another pastor's ministry. It's a free way to give yourself a break while having an opportunity to experience another's ministry firsthand.

It's really all about kingdom work, not church-kingdom work. It's not about growing our individual ministries or competing to be the best. It's about seeing teenagers' lives impacted for Christ regardless of whose church that happens in. The teamwork makes us much more effective than any of us could be on our own.

## Other Voices

**Bill Nance:**

It was good to read this, especially since our group of youth ministers just got done tonight with a huge community-wide service project. The teens in our groups dressed up as superheroes and went around town Trick-or-Treating for items for the food pantry. It was an awesome night. We collected a bunch of food, but we also got to share the gospel.

We do a lot of edifying and support. It's nice to know we're not alone in ministering for the kingdom of God and that we can help each other.

**Mike Kupferer:**

While I was in my first full-time ministry position, my network of youth workers kept me going through some difficult times. Even after I was gone from my position, I attended the meetings and spoke with the youth ministers. They were such a blessing to me, the ministry, and to all of my future students. I highly recommend starting a network if there's not one in your area.

**Justin Ross:**

If you're part of a denomination, do the same thing for all the churches of your denomination in your area. We'd not done this until about five years ago. While we don't meet as regularly as my local network does, it's another great asset and team to work with.

# 10 commandments for surviving in youth ministry

## 1. Thou shalt pray daily.

Are you picking up on this critical element to youth ministry yet? It's so important! Pray for personal issues, the ministry, your pastor, students, humility, and wisdom. It's absurd to think that we can effectively serve the Lord in ministry without discussing it with him on a regular basis. That's like working for a boss and never listening for direction, only it's not a business project at stake—it's a teenager's eternal destiny. We also need to be sure to spend time worshiping in prayer and listening to him in solitude. Some of my best prayer and worship moments are the times I finally stop talking to God and just listen, waiting for whatever he lays on my heart and mind.

## 2. Thou shalt regularly meditate on the Word.

The word meditate makes a lot of us uncomfortable because of the religious Eastern overtones, but the truth is we already know how to meditate. We just meditate on the wrong things. As Rick Warren said in *The Purpose Driven Life* (2002), "If you know how to worry, you already know how to meditate." Better to meditate on the Word than on the ministry complications that seem to be always present. Besides, how can we truly be the spiritual guides that teenagers need if we're not constantly traveling ahead on the journey ourselves? We need to spend more time preparing our own souls in the Word than we do preparing to instruct the souls of others. Only then will ministry come out of who we are rather than what we do.

## 3. Thou shalt always publicly respect and support your church's leadership.

After all, you're on the same team shepherding the same group of people. For the sake of building each other's credibility and avoiding gossip, take care of disagreements and conflict behind closed doors. If you argue in public, everyone loses: Gossip starts, people take sides, the body is divided, staff relationships are stressed, unity turns to tension, and prospective Christians leave the church because it's just as ugly in there as it is out in the world—except in the world people don't always fake it with smiles. If the conflict is severe enough, be willing to bow out graciously for the sake of the body and find employment elsewhere. Easier said than done, yes, but sometimes it's the most Christlike thing to do. Always make sure your disagreements are respectful and courteous and that discussions are limited to the person(s) involved.

## 4. Thou shalt get to know parents.

The more respect and trust the parents have for you, the more you'll be able to do (and get away with!) in ministry. You'll also create many opportunities for parents to share struggles and insights about their teenagers that will greatly benefit your ministry to those individuals. Prove yourself to be someone who cares about the family as a whole, not just the teens. Start conversations when parents drop off their teens or when they pick them up, even if you have to run out to the car to do so. Then, when a difficult time hits that family, they'll know whom they can come to and trust. Likewise, when a difficult time hits your ministry, they'll know your heart and you'll have their support.

## 5. Thou shalt invest in students' lives on an individual basis.

Don't assume someone else is doing it or that the teen doesn't really want it. Even in larger youth groups, pick a few teens and pour your life into them. If critics arise who accuse you of playing favorites, remember it's better to give a few teens individual godly attention than no one at all. Don't let the fear of critics paralyze your ministry. And if there are teens who are jealous and demand your time, that's great! Bring 'em on! Ensure that volunteers are doing the same with everyone else. Whatever you do, don't get so wrapped up in administrative tasks that there's no time for personal interaction with teens. Teens don't care what you do in the office all day or if your Sunday school lesson isn't too deep this week. If your actions don't prove that you have a personal interest in them, they won't be listening anyway.

## 6. Thou shalt evaluate criticism said privately in love.

Many people can see things you can't and have great insight into the ministry. Take heed and respond accordingly, but be careful about what's thrown around in gossip or said with a negative attitude. Don't let it discourage you from continuing to serve the Lord the best way you know. If it's said privately in love for the benefit of the ministry, then it might be worth listening to. The other stuff that's passed down through the grapevine by someone who's looking for attention can be evaluated, but don't let it sidetrack you from what is most important: serving the Lord by reaching teens for Christ.

## 7. Thou shalt communicate as often as possible.

Informed people are usually supportive people. Communicate well and often with your senior pastor, other staff members, parents, teens, volunteers, and your spouse. Sharing ideas and plans will eliminate a lot of unnecessary problems. Furthermore, communicating struggles and ministry complications with your pastor on a regular basis will save your back and maybe even protect your job when a situation blows up. It also builds trust and an atmosphere of teamwork. If you're not sure whether you're presently communicating enough, err on the side of too much communication (via a variety of methods) rather than find out later that it wasn't enough.

## 8. Thou shalt be flexible.

Small group discussions will go in more important directions than you originally anticipated, plans will change at the last minute, volunteers won't show up, and a thousand other things will remind you that you're not in control of your ministry. Be flexible when things change and approach these unforeseen situations with grace and a positive attitude. The Lord knows what he's doing and somehow—in the long run—it'll work out better than what you had in mind. Besides, it keeps you humble and reliant on him in all aspects of the ministry, which is the most important thing of all.

## 9. Thou shalt not be a solo act.

Don't build the ministry around yourself. If you do, the ministry will die when you leave. Focus on building and training solid volunteers who can do ministry just as effectively as you can. Function as an adult team leader even more than you function as a youth leader. You can't possibly reach every teen in your community, but with a strong team of qualified individuals, you can multiply yourself and your reach goes a lot further than it would otherwise. If you find that you do more than 80 percent of the total workload for your ministry, you're doing too much. For larger youth groups, that percentage should drop for you, too. Delegate. Train. Equip. Guide. And whatever you do, don't be a control freak. Give your volunteers the freedom to maybe not do as well as you could on their first or second try. (I find that most of them actually do better than I do!) The old cliché is true: Work yourself out of a job.

## 10. Thou shalt be thyself.

Don't be fake, extra cool, or someone you're not. Teens can smell a phony from miles away and will immediately discount you for it. They don't even care if you know all the latest music, have an outgoing personality, or if you're 60 years old. What they want is someone who's real, who's authentic and willing to be vulnerable, who admits weaknesses and mistakes, someone who's excited about them, and who's passionate about God. That's what teens want and that's what teens need. Be yourself. Everyone else is taken.

## Other Voices

### Kevin Twombly:

#6 is a great one. Whenever faced with criticism from a parent or friend I find myself praying that I would be open to learning anything that I need to learn through the experience.

### Tony Myles:

[Regarding #7]: Then there's the matter of communicating to people that they need to communicate, too.

### Kevin Twombly:

We've worked really hard on #9 to build a team-based ministry and through it have seen incredible effectiveness with lots of benefits:

- No burnout in our leaders because we all try to serve in our individual calling and passion.
- Unity with our whole leadership team because there's one common vision.
- No competition among leaders because we all strive to the same goal.
- Youth see the example and serve each other because they're seeing it modeled.

Team-based ministry is a win-win for everyone involved.

### Justin Ross:

I've been at my current church for nine years. It took me at least three years before I began to see the group come around and for it to become my own. This is when I finally began to see fruit from all of the hard work I had been doing. Many youth pastors give up just as they are rounding this corner. I'm not saying that everything magically changes, but I'm saying there are rewards for persevering and not giving up.

After nine years, there are nine teens either in full-time ministry or studying to go into ministry—not to mention the ones who have graduated from college, gotten married, and still love Jesus. That's pretty cool.

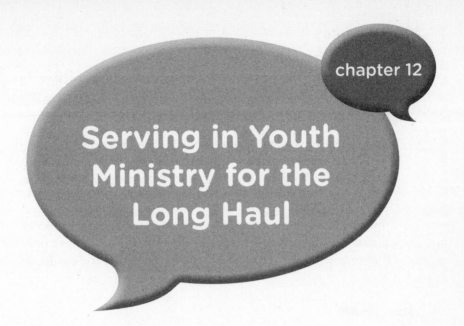

# chapter 12

# Serving in Youth Ministry for the Long Haul

## being versus doing

Identity in ministry should always precede function in ministry. Who you are in ministry determines what you do in ministry. Unfortunately—as the task-driven people we are—too many of us get that backward and focus on how our ministry functions rather than what it becomes. We look at what youth ministry should do while losing sight of what it should be, leaving us moving onto the next best curriculum, the next big event, and the next cool game that you hope will keep teens interested and involved.

It's easy to approach ministry from a doing perspective because it creates a sense of accomplishment at the end of the day when we're able to check several items off of the to-do list.

What if our youth ministries were known more for what they are rather than what they do? What if every teen in town knew our ministry as, "Yeah, that's the place where everyone feels loved and accepted," instead of, "Oh yeah, that's the church that goes on the ski trip every year, right?" Ski trips are fine, but we don't take ski trips just because that's what youth groups do—we go on ski trips because there's something about us that compels us to do it, whether that is the opportunity to connect with fringe students or the opportunity to take a small group of teens deeper into the Word for a weekend. The values of who we are as a ministry compel us to do what we do.

**Grahame Knox:**

I'll leave a couple of my favorite quotations, which have been instrumental in keeping me on the right track from time to time:

"The key to effective Christian youth work is people—people in whose lives Christ is alive, and who will open themselves to young people, not talk down to them, not dominate them with attractive personalities, but who show them how to love one another as Christ has commanded." (Mark Ashton, *Christian Youth Work*, Kingsway 1986.)

"The youth worker is not primarily a talker or organizer; he is a model, a person who by the power of his Christian example motivates a dedication to Jesus Christ." (Lawrence Richards, *Youth Ministry*, Zondervan 1972.)

**Shan Smith:**

Like balancing family and ministry, a healthy balance between being and doing is a necessity for anyone seeking longevity in ministry! This also seems to be one of the most difficult areas to achieve success in ministry.

# youth pastor is more than a title

A few weeks after a devastating earthquake hit Haiti on January 12, 2010, I went to the country to scout out missions opportunities for youth groups and also to brainstorm some relief efforts with Haitian pastors. Several other youth ministry bloggers were on the trip to help spread the word about a new opportunity to support the Haitian churches in the midst of the crisis.

Adam McLane, a one-time youth pastor who now works at Youth Specialties, was one of the bloggers on the trip. One afternoon he and I were sitting with one of our translators on the balcony of the house where we were staying. The translator asked me, "Are you a youth pastor?" I said yes. He turned to Adam and asked the same thing. Adam explained that he used to be a youth pastor, but now he works for Youth Specialties. Our translator pushed back and said that Adam is still a youth pastor even if he doesn't work at a church. Adam didn't really agree with him and, without missing a beat, our translator shot back, "You're always a pastor because being a pastor is your spiritual gift—not your title. Even if you don't work at a church, you're still a pastor."

I've been thinking about what he said. Being a pastor is not just a title we're assigned because we're paid staff at a church—it's also a spiritual gift (Ephesians 4:11). Here are two implications of this perspective:

- I went to school for seven years to learn how to use my spiritual gift of being a pastor/shepherd, but most of the things I spend my time doing each day are administrative tasks—a gift I don't have. I'd much rather be doing pastoral care for teens.
- More importantly, this means there are probably many more pastors in my church than I think—including teenagers. This puts a whole new spin on the term youth pastor. Right now, I'm neither intentionally using the youth pastors in my ministry, nor am I training them to do pastoral care in their schools and future work environments.

As I discussed in chapter 3, I think this will be part of the process of correcting the way I'm doing youth ministry all wrong. Instead of the ministry resting on my shoulders as the paid staff guy who provides a service for families in the church, it should be more about me equipping and training others to serve the rest of the body.

### Other Voices

**John Byrne:**
When you first told me this story, I started to think about how the words elder and pastor are interchangeable in Scripture. Of course this goes way beyond that. If the priesthood is for all believers, then it would make sense that on some level everyone would pastor.

Let me suggest that the position of pastor is an office, but the ability to pastor is a gift.

# how you will crash and burn(out) in ministry

I'm going to be honest: Every item I list here is based on tendencies I've noticed in myself. If you're a reader of my blog, maybe you've even noticed some of them pop up in my writing. When I take a step back and write about it, it's so easy to see how foolish I am. Burning out in ministry is not a sudden event in time that'll take me by surprise—like a firecracker on the 4th of July. Instead, it's a slow process over time—like holding a burning match. If I'm not careful, these things will eventually creep up on me, burn me, and render my leadership useless.

I doubt I'm alone in this. Here's how you and I will crash and burn(out) in ministry:

## 1. Ignore spending time in the Word and in prayer.

Ministry is easy—you can do it all in your own strength. It shouldn't be based on God anyway. Spend all your time teaching others how to develop their relationships with God instead.

## 2. Accept responsibility for everything.

Say yes to whatever is asked of you and your time. It doesn't matter if it could easily be handled by a volunteer—take it on anyway because you're the person they pay to do it. Besides, there may be no one else willing or available to do it other than you (which obviously indicates how important it is to everyone else).

## 3. Become emotionally attached to every situation.

Whenever someone has a need, be the first to jump in, provide all the emotional support they need, and rescue them from the problem. After all, everyone needs a savior—why shouldn't it be you?

## 4. Constantly serve God through ministry.

This is so important that you must sacrifice all personal downtime and fill it with good things like meetings, events, Bible studies, evangelism, mission trips, prayer groups, small groups, and knitting groups.

## 5. Attempt to control everything.

Control all the planning, the results, the future, the people, the workplace, the weather, and God. You're the sustainer of the ministry—the one on whom it's all built. If you take your eyes off of anything, it'll collapse and fail miserably.

## 6. Base your self-worth on the success of your ministry.

You're investing your life in this ministry thing. How it grows and flourishes indicates how important you are and how pleased God is with your labor. If your ministry is struggling, there must be something wrong with you.

## 7. Feed spiritual consumerism.

So-and-so left the church and is attending the megachurch down the street because they have a better youth ministry. Now you need to quickly compete by offering the same programs . . . only better. Otherwise, the entire congregation will migrate and leave you out of a job.

## 8. Focus your ministry on programs.

This may come as a result of the previous point. Remember that vision and relationships are secondary to programming. Look at Jesus, for example: His ministry was all about getting things done, not about growing disciples through relationships or communicating his vision for the world, right?

## 9. Dwell on all the problems.

So it turns out your ministry is the only one in the world that isn't perfect. Let it consume your thoughts, your heart, and your emotions. It's important to focus on internal problems so there's no time left to reach the lost souls who are dying all around.

## 10. Avoid transparency at all costs.

Vulnerability brings the potential for rejection, criticism, and people losing respect for you. As a church leader, everyone must think you're perfect, strong, and invincible. Otherwise, the perfect people in your church will have no reason to follow you.

## 11. Focus only on what's in front of you.

Dreaming a huge vision for the future only makes people feel uncomfortable (probably because of item #5). Passion can become contagious and take the ministry in scary and risky directions, so it's best to avoid these dreams altogether. It's always safer to wander aimlessly by staring at your feet than it is to walk toward God's beautiful horizon and risk tripping.

## Other Voices

### Claire Hailwood:

This is one of those posts that kind of pierces the heart because it makes me feel in equal measure uncomfortable because it's so real, and yet heartened because there are other youth workers out there wrestling with the same things. We become people who do rather than people who are all too often, but changing that in a way that affects the ministry is difficult because it means changing mindsets we see all around us and which are also probably deeply ingrained in us.

**Pete Leveson:**

This is good honest stuff that we need to hear. The only thing I think is missing (although it's kind of in #11) would be: "Go it alone—you don't need any help, or to be accountable, or people to come around and support you. You and God are enough!"

# avoiding burnout in ministry

Back in Bible college I had a professor whom I greatly admired and respected for his knowledge of Scripture and its implementation in real life ministry. What I respected most was his openness and honesty about his life, both the successes and all the failures. Throughout my four years in college, his constant advice was clear, "Establish your boundaries and place your family first—there'll always be more to do." This advice comes from a man who started strong in pastoral ministry but eventually burned out due to overwork and neglect of his family's needs.

Through hearing his stories in college and then hearing the same advice frequently repeated in seminary, setting ministry boundaries was something that was ingrained in me. Back then, I gave the time to God that belongs to him and took time for myself without feeling guilty about it. Over time, however, those boundaries slowly started to erode—not necessarily because of pressure to perform, but because I passionately love ministry.

But in order to have a family and survive in ministry, time restrictions must be established and kept. There will always be more work to do, meetings to attend, demands to be met, people to reach, and planning to complete. And there will also always be tomorrow to work on those things. And, if tomorrow never comes, then apparently God didn't think those things were important enough to complete anyway.

## Other Voices

### Len Evans:

Here is a dirty little secret about ministry: Hardly anyone is going to ask you about the condition of your soul. If you don't look out for your own spiritual and physical health, nobody else will. And when—not if—you burn out, they'll grieve for a period and replace you within six months. Avoid the pain by guarding your time and your soul.

## Ryan Nielsen:

If you're married, make sure you have a regular date night and make this sacred! My wife and I decided to do this weekly when we got married. Now that we have two children, we realize that the date night can't happen weekly, but my wife knows that my day off is sacred for time with my family. Or course there's the occasional real emergency (a student is in a car accident, a teen just found out her parents are getting a divorce, and so on) that does need my attention on my day off. But there are also teen-perceived emergencies (a teen's girlfriend just broke up with him, a girl's parents won't let her go to the party Friday night, and so on), which don't need immediate attention and can be dealt with the next working day. If you're going to avoid burnout, you need to keep time for your family sacred. And you need to take time for yourself as well.

## Tony Myles:

Consider the following:

- How many nights this past week did you go to bed at a reasonable hour?
- What day is your cell phone turned off?
- When you're online, do you constantly feel the need to check your email and social networking sites . . . to the point where you're not getting any work done?
- Where in your life are you simply a person who's following God versus being a youth worker?
- Who are your friends outside of your ministry?
- Why did you break your last weekly Sabbath (if you even have a weekly Sabbath)?

Of course, you probably have good reasons for some of the awkward answers you might come up with to those questions. At least, that may be what you're telling yourself.

## Lars Rood:

I've got a long history of being opinionated about this subject. In my years of youth ministry I've always worked at large churches with large youth staffs and volunteer teams. This is an area that I teach on in trainings. It's very easy to tell which people on your staff will burn out: They're the ones who never take care of themselves. They work too many hours, have few friends outside of youth ministry, are always with teens, and never say no.

## how to leave a youth ministry position well

No one wants to think about the day they'll have to leave their ministry, but unless we're raptured or have a plan for avoiding death, we'll all one day leave our ministries whether we like it or not. One day we'll all be replaced.

When that day comes, it's wise to think through the transition so that you can leave well. Here are several things to consider:

### Don't make promises you won't, can't, or shouldn't keep.

For example, "I'll come back and visit you all," or, "You can still call me whenever you want." Students will cling to these statements emotionally and be hurt again in the future when they're not fulfilled. If you're planning to visit again next year on vacation or something, that's fine, but don't tell them that just so they'll feel better. Do your best to make a clean break for the sake of the ministry and the next person who takes the position.

### Decide which of your responsibilities must continue and delegate them to volunteers.

If possible, take a week or two to overlap your involvement in these areas to ensure a smooth transition.

### Listen to everyone.

There'll be many different responses to your departure. It's not important that you address every concern (or expression of relief!), but rather that everyone feels heard, respected, and valued.

### Once you leave, it's hands off.

Don't contact people to see if you're missed or indulge those who contact you with some follow-up work or complaints. And when a new person takes over and teens contact you about how it's different (because it will be), always encourage them to be positive and support the new leader.

### Never publicly bad-mouth anyone.

This is especially true if you're leaving with tension. You don't have to support various decisions and people, but don't tear the ministry apart even further just so you feel like you've had the final say and gotten your revenge. That doesn't mean you should avoid issues and be dishonest with the church leadership—but leave with grace.

## Other Voices

### Scott Aughtmon:

When I left a former youth ministry, I said straight out, "I want you to like the next leader as much, if not more than me. That won't hurt me! I don't want you to be mad at the next person and blame them for me leaving. I'm leaving because I feel that God's leading me—it's not because of the new youth pastor. And it's not because anything's wrong with you or this church. If you reject the new youth pastor and attack him because I left and he ends up leaving, I still won't be back. I can't, because I know it's my time to leave. The way to make me (and God) happy is to keep growing together, grow closer to God, and submit to the next leader." I wanted the group to last and not collapse when I left. If and when I ever heard from teens about the "new guy" I always was happy when things were going well, and I always defended him.

### Mike Kupferer:

The most important thing to remember when leaving a ministry is that integrity is vital. Don't do or say anything that'll damage or ruin your integrity. You're a child of God first, and full-time employee afterward.

# Conclusion

I know that some of you feel like your investment in the lives of teens is worthless—you're seeing absolutely no growth, no life change. Some of you are frustrated, tired, struggling, and wondering, "Is all this time, energy, and emotion worth it?"

Last weekend I received this Facebook message from a girl I haven't been in touch with for about a decade. For the sake of her privacy, I edited out some of the details and have permission to share it with you to encourage you as you work with teenagers.

> Tim, you knew me 10 years ago by my maiden name. I'm not sure if you remember me. I just wanted to say thank you. Thank you for being my friend! Most of all, thank you for striving to truly live your faith and for not being ashamed to do so. You lived your life in a distinctly different manner from all my other friends, and it made an impression on me. Adolescence was a rough season of my life. There were a couple of people in my life during that time who were "Jesus with skin on," and you were one of them. I'm sure you've continued to be a blessing to teens through your ministry and life. Now I'm a pastor's wife (whoa!). My husband was ordained last year and we're blessed with two little boys, ages two years and four months. I stumbled upon your website a few months ago while helping my husband look up info on youth groups, and I realized how God had blessed me through you, and I wanted you to know.

Not every teenager will come back and thank you. In fact, just like the 10 lepers in Luke 17:11-19, most won't. But the ones who do will remind you that the sweat, energy, and tears are a small price to pay for the eternal impact the Lord left on that teen's life through you.

As you're ministering to and investing in teenagers, keep Jesus' ministry in mind: His Father gave him a specific mission, and I'm sure we all agree that he had an incredibly successful ministry—but, for as many people as he taught, healed, and challenged, even more people were left unhealed, unchallenged, and untaught. Almost every day he passed by communities full of people who needed the blessing of his time and attention.

Jesus didn't try to do it all.

Neither should your ministry.

Most of us will read this and intellectually agree, but far too many of us are acting like we're greater than Jesus, while leading ministries that are trying to outperform him.

Whether it's self-inflicted or not, relieve yourself of the pressure to lead your ministry in too many directions. Determine the vision God's equipped your ministry to best pursue. Know that mission. Focus on it. Let nothing deter you from it—not even other ministry opportunities.

Even though you may never see it, the fruit is worth the labor. God has called you to minister to teens and has created you to fulfill that mission in a specific way no one else can. You can't be a spiritual influence for every teen out there, but you can influence some, and you may never know the influence you have on a teen just by being present in his or her life.

God bless you for your "life in student ministry," lived for him and his teenagers.

# Acknowledgments

## Thank you to the online youth ministry community!

This book would never have been written without the tremendous support, encouragement, and wisdom of youth workers from all over the world who have poured into me through Facebook, Twitter, YouTube, and their blogs. Thank you all for your amazing contribution to the content of this book and for your ongoing dedication to invest in youth workers like me!

I must say thank you especially to—

Bill Allison, Mike Andrews, Nick Arnold, Scott Aughtmon, Ben Bacon, Phil Bell, Steve Blanchard, Paul Bowman, Matt Brown, Dave Burkholder, D.J. Butcher, John Byrne, Josh Christian, Adam Walker Cleaveland, Cindy Coker, Trent Cornwell, Tom Cottar, Dan Crouch, Steve Cullum, Jason Curlee, Dare2Share Ministries, Glenn W. Davies, Chris Day, Joel Diaz, Jon Eagleson, Brian Eberly, Ruth Elkin, Grant English, Sara Evanchick, Len Evans, Gerald Faulkner, Mike Ferber, Rob Finkill, Brian Ford, Josh Frank, Dave Furst, Kyle Galle, Patti Gibbons, Aaron Giesler, Jenna Gilbertson , Rob Gillen, Chris Goeppner, Jeff Graham, Eric Groezinger, Claire Hailwood, Matt Hall, Jeremy Hallquist, Eric Helton, Brett Hetherington, Erica Hoagland, Lantz Howard, Jason Huffman, Jason Hughlett, Jeremy Isaacs, Gregg Jacobs, Chuck Jespersen, Brandon Johns, Tom Kay, Sunnie Kim, Brian Kirk, Grahame Knox, Mike Kupferer, Pete Leveson, Paul Martin, Benjer McVeigh, Lynn Mills, Terry Moore, Mike Morris, Jordan Muck, Tony Myles, Mike Nagel, Bill Nance, Ryan

Nielsen, Calvin Park, Matt Parker, Ryan Peduzzi, David Plumley, Corey Potter, Tom Pounder, Roy Probus, Lars Rood, Tony Roos, Justin Ross, Ebere Samuel, Jason Sansbury, Stephen Sarine, Dana Schmoyer, David Schmoyer, Jerry Schmoyer, Waldy Schröder, Brenda Seefeld, Jeff Smith, Shan Smith, Lori Still, EJ Swanson, Luke Trouten, Paul Turner, Kevin Twombly, Shane Vander Hart, Justin Van Rheene, Zac Wheeler, PJ Wong, Franklin Wood, Jeff Wright, Shane Yancey, Troy Young, and Jeremy Zach.

## Share Your Thoughts

**With the Author:** Your comments will be forwarded to the author when you send them to *zauthor@zondervan.com*.

**With Zondervan:** Submit your review of this book by writing to *zreview@zondervan.com*.

## Free Online Resources at

## www.zondervan.com

**Zondervan AuthorTracker:** Be notified whenever your favorite authors publish new books, go on tour, or post an update about what's happening in their lives at www.zondervan.com/authortracker.

**Daily Bible Verses and Devotions:** Enrich your life with daily Bible verses or devotions that help you start every morning focused on God. Visit www.zondervan.com/newsletters.

**Free Email Publications:** Sign up for newsletters on Christian living, academic resources, church ministry, fiction, children's resources, and more. Visit www.zondervan.com/newsletters.

**Zondervan Bible Search:** Find and compare Bible passages in a variety of translations at www.zondervanbiblesearch.com.

**Other Benefits:** Register yourself to receive online benefits like coupons and special offers, or to participate in research.

ZONDERVAN®

ZONDERVAN.com/
AUTHORTRACKER
*follow your favorite authors*